Emergence:

Baudelaire

Mallarmé

Rimbaud

Emergence:

Baudelaire

Mallarmé

Rimbaud

CYRIL and LILIANE WELCH

Bald Eagle Press

Copyright   1973

Bald Eagle Press / State College, Pa.

L. C. Catalog Card Number 72-96845

Printed in the United States of America

Designed by Eleanore Rubin

Preface

The last few decades have borne witness to a change of climate in the world of poetry. There has been a general rejection of most of the traditional forms and styles, accompanied by a good deal of experimentation. One often gets the impression, however, that the experimentation is a bit frenzied, a bit frantic. For the change of climate has meant predominantly a removal of the usual safeguards of poetry once enjoyed by the poet. At various times and places, poetry could be justified in terms of its ability to entertain or edify. But today there seems to be a general uneasiness about whether these functions define the poetic work. Indeed, we sometimes hear it said that one or the other, entertainment or edification, has no place whatsoever in poetry. In whatever way we construe the problem, it all comes down to saying that we today need a refreshed, if not a new understanding of poetry, of what poems are and might be.

The task of achieving a renewed understanding of anything is too great to be completed at any given moment. For the task belongs to a generation and an epoch. However, it can and must be approached in several different ways. One way is to assume that previous generations or epochs contained the kernel of thought which has since been unfolding into the present predicament, into a situation that is both a potential and a crisis. But even if this assumption is made, it still remains to ask where the kernel of thought is to be found.

We look back to nineteenth-century French poetry, to Baudelaire, Mallarmé, and Rimbaud for the first radical break with traditional styles of poetry.

Charles Baudelaire (1821-1867) was one of the first to embody in his work the poetry of modernity. His volume of poems *Les Fleurs du mal* (1857) was sufficiently outrageous to bring down upon him a court trial; he was fined 300 francs and ordered to withdraw six poems from the work. In 1864 he published *Spleen de Paris*, a collection of prose poems. In 1868 appeared posthumously his most important theoretical writings, *Curiosités esthétiques and L'Art romantique*. Baudelaire's poetry and his many short treatises on art helped develop the thought that poetry could no longer be simply the play of imagination in a purely eternal realm, divorced from history. Instead, poetry was seen to arise out of the depths of human existence as it unfolded in a particular cultural context defined by varying human needs and efforts.

Stéphane Mallarmé (1842-1898) began writing poetry in 1862. From then until his death he rewrote his verse, carefully extracting all syntactic elements that would open it to facile understanding. The first version of his collected poems *Poésies* appeared in 1887, the posthumous version in 1898. His most innovative legacy to the future was *"Un Coup de dés jamais n'abolira le hasard,"* a twenty-two page calligram which introduced a revolutionary typographical arrangement of the scattered text on the double page. Like his predecessor Baudelaire, Mallarmé also engaged in translations of Edgar Allan Poe. He was also a critic. His interpretations of literary pieces, music performances, and ballets are contained in *Divagations* (1897) along with his prose poems. What is most distinctive about his writings whether in verse or prose is their obscurity. Hermetic, his works brought to the fore a new understanding of language and a new concept of poetry. Following Baudelaire's dictum that poetry was an "evocatory witchcraft," Mallarmé elevated poetry to pure suggestiveness.

Arthur Rimbaud (1854-1891) had written all of his poetic creations by the time he was nineteen. After *Une Saison en enfer* (1872) and *Les Illuminations* (1872-73), he ceased writing poetry and embarked on a life of adventure and wandering. His prophetic statements on his own poetic program and the practices of future poets are contained in "Les Lettres du voyant," two letters written by the seventeen-year old boy to his teachers. Mallarmé's description of Rimbaud as "an exiled angel" and "a meteor" suggests the dynamic, explosive, and revolutionary character of Rimbaud's poetry. The prose poems Les Illuminations violate not only the French tradition of prosody but also introduce a form of bounded chaos hitherto absent from poetry.

Although the lives of these poets make interesting reading, their true contribution emerges in its fullest force in their works. By focusing on specific poems and by looking at key theoretical writings, we have tried to elicit their conception of the experience of art. Since the approach itself is here at issue, the first essay speaks directly to the questions, What is literature? and What is criticism? in an attempt to formulate a view of what it means to undertake and fulfill the task of literary criticism.

reflections on literary criticism

I

Most human endeavors have been called into question. Our century is an iconoclastic age wherein old gods have been dethroned, established ideas and new ideologies quickly emptied of their initial meaning. Moreover, it is becoming increasingly difficult to fill the void left by the retreat of these absolutes of the past.

Literary criticism is a hybrid literature, taking its stand somewhere between creative writing and philosophical thought. This peculiarity of its nature has always made it especially vulnerable to scorn if not attack by poets and philosophers alike, each looking upon the efforts of the critic as falling short of their standards. Thus the discipline of literary criticism—or what we would rather call literary interpretation—is ever needy of revaluation and reconsideration. Nowadays, though, much dissatisfaction with nearly all accepted procedures of human inquiry makes it particularly relevant to become thoughtfully self-critical as well as critical, and to try out alternative approaches to literature rather than simply to become entrenched in those that are establishd. For we can no longer assume that what is established will for that reason also be acceptable.

Few are those who have ever been able to maintain, unaided, their effort to penetrate to the depths of the literature which eventually came to sustain them. Literature of continuing significance generally requires some sort of mediation: the contagious enthusiasm of a teacher, the sometimes confusing interpretations of friends, the systematic interpretations of a critic. In ancient times the rhapsodes recited the poetry of Homer and others, enlivening their recitation with mime: they actually embodied the meaning and so directly involved their audience. They spoke not as a second party to their audience and as a third party to the poem. The recitation itself was an event, one in which the rhapsode, the poet, the poem, and the audience—perhaps the nation and the prevailing culture—came together at a unique moment and were what they were by virtue of the event of that moment. Nowadays, however, criticism (literally, the effort to bring the human spirit to the point of crossing the line from opacity to translucency) oscillates between meeting the demands of academic scholarship and fulfilling the needs of anonymous journalism: on the one hand, a mass of observed detail concealing a value judgment or a value judgment obscuring careful observation and participation; on the other hand, a flamboyant "explanation" trying either to promote or to squelch the latest works in art, but in any event popularizing them into accessible formulations.

There are critics who have risen to the challenge, each in his own way: G. Bachelard, R. Barthes, M. Blanchot, J. Starobinski, J.-P. Richard, G. Poulet, E. Staiger, and no doubt a handful more. Different as each is from the others, they share a common concern: to return the interpretation of literature to a more thoughtful terrain, where it is neither confined within academic concerns nor committed to addressing a populace whose only wish is to be "cultured" or *au courant*. They draw upon both poetic and philosophic literature, evidencing not only a sensitivity for the one but also an insight into the other. As for their philosophical lineage, the German thinker Martin Heidegger has contributed more than any other single man to the formation of their principles. Heidegger exemplifies the manner in which his thought can bring us toward literature in his interpretations of the poet Hölderin especially (*Erläuterungen zu Hölderlins Dichtung*) but in his interpretations of other poets also (*Unterwegs zur Sprache*). The principle underlying his interpretations is expressed in a figure:

> In the din of "unpoetic languages" poems are like a bell suspended out in the open and already out of tune owing to the light snowfall coming down upon it . . . . Perhaps every interpretation of these poems is a snowfall upon the bell. Whatever then an interpretation may be able to do, or unable to do, one

thing can be said about it: in order that what has been formed in and by the poem may stand before us a bit more clearly, the interpretative discourse must always dissolve both itself and its own designs. For the sake of what has been poetically formed, the interpretation of the poem must strive to make itself superfluous. The last and also the most difficult step of any exposition consists in this: to vanish, along with its interpretations, in the face of what stands before us in and by virtue of the poem itself. . . . Accordingly, when we read the poems over again we feel as though we had already at the start understood them that way. It is well if we come to feel this.[1]

The principle of literary interpretation is paradoxical. The critic has to do something: he must speak, analyze, form his own argument, and say something. And yet, even supposing that the critic has overcome the temptations to parade his own cleverness or has condescended to serve an indifferent public, he still has to let the poem speak for itself. The rhapsodes resolved the paradox by giving themselves up to the poem in body and in soul. The character of modern thinking, however, prevents us from abandoning ourselves in this way. When we speak, we do so as individuals, for better or for worse; we cannot identify our speech with that of the nation. According to Heidegger's figure, though, the problem is not one of how to break the silence and say something. The problem is rather that the din of "unpoetic languages" distorts what poetic language has to say for itself. In positive terms, then, the problem for the critic is to speak in a way that hushes "fallen" language, not by calling attention to the inadequacies of ordinary speech but by focusing attention upon what the poem has to say, purely and simply. The paradox of course remains. It can only be resolved, and then only tenuously, in the actual undertakings of interpretation. But nevertheless it is well to bear it in mind.

II

In the first part of the last century Hegel writes that art was and would remain a thing of the past. This judgment claims that art can never again be the living force it once was in our lives, even if it is well executed and effectively mediated by teachers, friends, and critics. The claim is part of Hegel's conception of history and of the development of the human spirit, wherein all modes of thought and action are transcended and retained only as transcended. The full statement is:

> In all these respects art is and shall remain, as far as its highest meaning for us goes, a thing of the past. It has therewith also lost, for us, its genuine veracity and vivacity, and becomes instead something we think more about than something that could ever assert its earlier necessity and assume its higher place in reality.[2]

When Hegel says "all these respects," he is referring to his own historical account: Art is first of all limited to sensuous embodiment of meaning for man. For the Greeks, art was above all a thing of the present; they experienced the meaning of their own experience and of the world directly in the sensuous medium as it was immediately presented to them in their sculptures, their plays, their recitations of Homer. In the Middle Ages, with the advent of Christianity, meaning (truth) for man was conceived in terms that in principle, though not always in fact, transcended the sensuous. If the Christian saw in the architecture of his cathedral a meaning for his life, it was strangely allegorical, a sensuous portrayal of something else, namely, the spiritual. Now today, for the modern mind, even this submission to the allegorical has become something of an impossibility. We insist on figuring things out, thinking about them, coming to terms with meanings in a reflective manner, and withholding our consent to immerse ourselves in these meanings until they have been checked out. Since we are not able to give ourselves up directly to the sensuous, we find we are debarred from the immediacy essential to the fullest experience of art. It is not the artist's public alone but the artist himself, living within the thought patterns of his particular age and necessarily partaking of them, who inevitably reflects upon his own undertakings and thereby removes himself from immediate involvement in the mode of meaning peculiar to art.

Art still has, Hegel says, a "highest meaning" for us. Art in a particular manner embodies subjective spirit in objective circumstances, whereby spirit fulfills itself by becoming also its otherness. The otherness in this case is the sensuous. But then art is a bridge which we have historically crossed. Hegel's concept of history, though, entails repetition: any truly historical development lives on as a development. What is transcended in the development is retained as transcended. Thus, even if we have crossed the bridge of the sensuous, of art, this bridge has become one of the number which must be simultaneously crossed. But nowadays when we cross it, we know also what should be happening in any given case and thereby insist on assuring ourselves reflectively that this particular bridge is indeed suitable for crossing. When we listen to a concert or experience its resonance afterwards, we not only *enjoy* it, as Hegel goes on to say, but we also *judge* it according to whether it is fulfilling its established function. As something in essence established, it is something of the past.

Although art, as a familiar part of our experience rather than a source of its meaning, is already established and therefore known, we may still lose our bearings when we find ourselves on the high seas. Unlike Columbus, we know what is there, but this knowledge does not in itself insure safe passage. At the very least, all such seas must be charted and all the variables of the voyage carefully studied. As soon as we have knowledge (*Wissen*) of something, that something is of the past. The task of the future, then, is to preserve the meaning of this knowledge by systematizing it, by turning it into what Hegel calls science (*Wissenschaft*). Thus Hegel ends the same paragraph, which began by claiming art to be a thing of the past, by remarking:

> For this reason a *science* of art is much more urgently
> needful in our time than in those times when art by
> itself, as art, provided complete satisfaction. Art invites
> us to thoughtful contemplation—not, to be sure, for
> the purpose of calling it forth once again, but rather
> for the purpose of ascertaining scientifically what art
> is.[3]

Art is a thing of the past not because it is outdated, nor because it is now fully understood and filed away for occasional reference, nor because it no longer affects us in a vital way. Rather, art is a thing of the past precisely because it has a well established place which needs to be understood since it now affects us powerfully and inconspicuously.

Quite apart from Hegel's broader metaphysical scheme, much of what he specifically says has achieved a factual basis. Art has assumed a twofold appearance. 1) We look to art for a diversion from our ordinary routines, not a celebration of human experience but a distraction of the mind, an amusement which anesthetizes us for a span of time intervening between more "serious" endeavors. We watch movies which border on gossip, musicals which sing away our sorrows, television programs which afford a peek into the lives of others or into far away lands. We are in this case suspicious of elements requiring effort to understand or implying any direct relationship with the graver exigencies of life. 2) We look to art for culture, and of course then prefer to regard it as "great" art, long accepted as perfected and expressive of higher humanistic and technical values. We visit museums and archives, pull out the tools and standards of scholarship, and probably expect to be paid for our efforts once we no longer have to listen to those who are. This second aspect of art understandably gives rise to the first: once art requires tedious inquiry to appreciate its "message" or "exquisiteness," we naturally look to the exact opposite for relief. Hegel calls the resultant oscillation a form of alienation. A century later John Dewey describes it thus:

> So extensive and subtly pervasive are the ideas that set Art upon a remote pedestal, that many a person would be repelled rather than pleased if told that he enjoyed his casual recreations, in part at least, because of their esthetic quality. The arts which today have most vitality for the average person are things he does not take to be art: for instance, the movie, jazzed music, the comic strip, and, too frequently, newspaper accounts of love-nests, murders, and exploits of bandits. For when what he knows as art is relegated to the museum and gallery, the unconquerable impulse toward experiences enjoyable in themselves finds such outlet as the daily environment provides.[4]

Similarly artists, particularly poets, have allowed their works to become permeated with reflective intention. Proust, for example, writes a series of novels which also embody thoughts upon the significance of writing in the understanding of temporal meanings. Some artists concentrate so much on the significance of their own work that they seem to work mainly for themselves. Others insist upon the prominence of a "message," perhaps some social evil and its reform. And still others devote their works to prove the singular point that art need have no message but somehow transcends all meaning. The National Film Board of Canada has produced a film that shows nothing more or less than a group of youngsters conversing in meandering and broken phrases about the significance of a film they have just seen. Art that does not sell its imitations on the entertainment market has become its own critic.

What is happening here? Basically, the human experience of meaning has been bifurcated into two distinct realms, the subjective and the objective. An art work initially stimulates a man so that he experiences or feels a meaningful moment. In order to linger on the experience, this same man—a scholar perhaps—inquires into its "nature." This inquiry proceeds objectively, since the subjective experience is taken to be adequate to itself if not complete. To be objective here means to specify observable features of the art object and of the human subject, trying in the end to relate the resultant manifold of detail to the original now rather remote feeling. The twain shall never meet, of course. The inquiry itself is only objective relative to its subject; in essence it is expressive of the peculiar leanings of the inquirer, that is, it is subjective. Reflection is then as subjective as the original feeling. Modern psychology supports this popular view for the purposes of everyday affairs, and the history of philosophy over the last few centuries (with Hegel as a star contributor) supports the academic view for more theoretical endeavors. Reflection, so construed, does not basically deepen the original experience or even fathom its initial depth. Reflection here emphasizes — not necessarily underscores theoretically, but rather embodies directly—the individuality of the human subject. "After all," we would like to say of ourselves as well as of others, "it is just a matter of taste . . . of feeling . . . of preference . . . " Such a comment belittles the individual's experience only in appearance. It intimates that what counts above all else in art—and in other domains as well—is critical skepticism, evaluation, or affirmation of the individual in the face of objective circumstances. We witness here the self-assertion of the human subject rather than the manifestation of the world in which he lives.

If we do not overcome this metaphysic of subjectivity, art will become for us "something of the past" in the more facile and ultimately disastrous sense. As soon as art works are taken unequivocally and absolutely as stimulants for subjective feeling or objective research, they will not only be deprived of any intrinsic power or relevance but they will also be rapidly replaced by more efficacious stimulants—drugs, for instance. In a similar context Heidegger writes that the death of art will occur precisely because we insist on taking "lived experience" (*Erlebnis*) as the unchangeable core of our involvement in art and add to this our objective inquiry.[5]

If we are to overcome the alienation and its portent, we will have to accept two principles. First, we will have to accept and acknowledge the element of reflection within the work of art, the involvement of both the artist and the appreciator in it. For Hegel is right when he notes that modern man's involvement in anything requires above all "self-consciousness": an awareness and an account of one's own stand with regard to the meanings one experiences. But art cannot survive simply as an occasion for the self-assertion of the human subject—and neither can the human subject. Art is the manifestation of the world in which we live. Second, we will have to accept and acknowledge that art always brings forth an otherness which cannot be reduced to human reflection and yet localizes the meanings we then articulate reflectively. Taken separately and one at a time, these two principles offer nothing new nor very challenging. Taken together, they appear mutually incompatible, since it has long been understood that reflection reduces meaning to subjective terms, while anything truly other than man, over against man—even the world in which he lives—has long been construed to be empty of meaning. There is a challenge, then, and at this moment of history it is a formidable one.

As a mediator, the critic must learn a way to bring out the reflective strain in art while at the same time allowing the meaning of this strain to emerge as contrapuntal to what reflective man confronts. This way cannot be taught or defended in advance. Examples of it are the only instructions in it and the only arguments for it.

III

Whatever we are doing or undertaking, questions occur to us which transcend the daily detail and pertain to the significance of the whole. As literary critics we find ourselves asking such questions as, What is literature? How does literature achieve the power it does in the thoughts and lives of men? Why do writers write and readers read? Such questions may appear idle, irrelevant, or abstract when we are immersed in the detail that arises in working out our assigned tasks. The way we answer these questions, however, determines in total measure the tasks we deem to be significant, the detail we judge to be relevant, and the standards by which we evaluate our results. If these questions are not asked, it is simply because the answers have been assumed.

The disturbing peculiarity of the question, What is literature? is that it seems to be unanswerable. A question about some detail within an undertaking can usually be defined, the subject investigated, and an answer formulated in a way that puts an end to the question. A question about the undertaking itself, however, not only eludes any proposed definition of the criteria for a final solution but it also disrupts the flow of the undertaking, suspending the claims entailed by the tasks involved and leaving us idle. It is often argued that pondering questions about the overall meaning of an undertaking might easily terminate the undertaking. We must realize, however, that the question What is literature? arises differently than "detail" questions. There are no final answers or solutions, not because it is so difficult and obscure but because it serves to guide us to new modes of literature and new ways of responding to literature. The question places us at the threshold; without it we would settle ourselves in the waiting-room. And to the objection that we cannot ask a genuine question unless we envisage the definite possibility of a final answer to it, the reply must be that to any genuine question which we might ask, the answer comes upon us, and we respond in kind. We do not really ask those questions which we have simply chosen to ask.

Then, what about literature? What can profitably be thought about the written works of literary artists "in general"— poems, novels, or plays—apart from what might be thought about particular works? We could no doubt mention and develop any number of characteristics, factual or normative: Literature is instruction (in morals, in religion, in history, in social mores); entertainment (to distract or to rejuvenate the mind with pleasant images); exercise (in the finer nuances of a language); excitation (to undertake action, to become conscious of ourselves or of nature). It is, however, hardly incidental that we are never really satisfied with any of these characteristics elevated to the status of a principle. The moment we "get into" a particular work, something else happens which renders all theses characteristics secondary and ornamental. This something else is *conflict*. We are ripped away from the surface, namely, from our ordinary and familiar ways of thinking, feeling, and acting—at first perhaps unwillingly, but then eventually with gratitude—thrust down into the depths of the particular work itself. Yet we do not simply arrive, nor are we ever in a position to experience the depths in their purity; these are only wishful dreams occasioned sometimes by art. Instead we experience the absolute difference between the surface of life with which we are very familiar and the depth intimated as a possibility. As a result we are cast into the thick of the conflict from which we do not emerge unscathed. From this conflict we might be instructed, amused, exercised, or excited, but apart from it we will be demoralized, dissipated, fatigued, or anesthetized.

Stéphane Mallarmé, who speaks elliptically about his art and its significance, formulates the point in "Le Mystère dans les lettres":

> There must after all be something occult in everybody's heart; I am a firm believer in something abstruse and significant, closed up and hidden away in commonplace things: For as soon as the mob gets a whiff of the possibility that what is obscure is a reality—something, for example, on a sheet of paper in some written work, but not in itself—it gets all worked up, a jealous hurricane anxious to attribute the darkness to anything whatsoever, all thunder and lightning. (M, 383)

Mallarmé thus interprets generously the indignation commonly aroused by the suggestion that something eluding one's comprehension might after all be of prime significance. He sees this anger caused by the unmanifested yet very real profundity in all men, as this profundity is brought out into the open by what lurks in apparently harmless things. In other words, the sparks that fly upon contact with literature argue for a depth common to both men and literature. The literary work of art is, on the face of it, just one more trivial manifestation on the surface of human experience. And yet suddenly it reveals a great depth which, from the surface, shows merely darkness and obscurity and which can be so frightening as to prevent all further exploration.

Another example is the once famous counterthesis known as Plato's Complaint. For Plato as for any Greek, poetic endeavors were central rather than peripheral to human experience. He formulated various theories on poetry in several dialogues, most famously in his *Republic,* where the poets are censured on the grounds that their works endanger the human spirit. As one reads the other dialogues, one discovers that the Complaint contains the germ of a Compliment. The power Plato ascribes to the poetic work turns out to be fundamental: it brings us to the inspired madness requisite for piercing the surface of things. Poets are too much like philosophers to be tolerated wherever philosophers rule. However, the poetic work falls short of philosophical discourse in only one important respect: after piercing the surface of human experience it leaves us suspended over the abyss, giving us no hint (as Plato's dialogues do) of a clearly defined reality at the bottom of the dark pit. Thus poetic literature endangers us with anarchy, since it breaks the spell of the ordinary without committing us to its origin. Plato felt that to maintain the spell of the ordinary by an elaborate system of "noble lies" was better than to expose the uninitiated to the dangers of uncontrolled and incomplete revelations.

Mallarmé and Plato agree on one salient point: literature breaks the surface of quiet waters and thereby reveals obscurity. Literature also makes clear that this obscurity is the source of multifarious possibilities.

A literary work of art places us in the thick of a conflict; it does not theoretize about it. It draws us into its own articulation by conjuring up familiar ways of thinking, feeling, and acting. We recognize the meanings thus articulated, find ourselves at home in the articulation: we recognize ourselves in it. A failed work stops short right here: for example, newspaper stories or comic book adventures or soapbox operas give us pleasure by distracting us from our own troubles or boredoms. The truly dynamic work of art, however, has just begun. With a firm hold upon us, the work proceeds to transform rather than confirm our prevalent mode of experience. Our thoughts, feelings, and actions, instead of remaining intact as they usually do, take on another dimension of meaning, sometimes positive and sometimes negative. Transfigured at the outset by the very form of the work, they now receive from the artistry of the poet another interpretation, a new content. However, the content of the work does not become part of our ordinary or extraordinary personal and cultural baggage. It remains in opposition to us. We experience it as providing a momentary support which presents itself *for*, and yet remains always different *from*, our person and our culture. If we fully absorb the work, it no longer means anything to us as literature but becomes just one more item in our baggage of half-meanings.

A literary work which can be reduced to a thesis often disappoints us because it leaves us with excess baggage, the meaning of which is still suspect. Instead of focusing our thoughts, feelings, or actions on an alien content, such a work uses possible content, the subject matter presented, to confirm the thought, feeling, or action proposed. Only so long as familiar meanings relate to content alien to them, only so long as they remain transparently relative, is human experience consummated. In a technical sense, then, it is the function of art, and above all linguistic art (since language is man's most fundamental mode of existence), to "reduce" all theses (all familiar or possibly familiar meanings) to a content which both completes and opposes those meanings.

Literary art opens up new vistas. This opening, though, does not confirm old familiar or new additional meanings. It is the opening of all such meanings upon an alien content. But what is the content of the new vistas? Particular works of art "answer" this question, each in its own way and at its own time. A theoretical answer to the question must remain "provisional," it must allow the work itself to present its content in its own terms. Such a provisional answer has in effect already been given. If a novel, say, brings together and articulates a manifold of meanings (familiar thoughts, feelings, and actions), it is recalling human interpretation of *what* things are, *what* situations mean to us, *what* we may do about circumstances. If the same novel (or poem or play) opens these meanings out upon alien content (not just adding or confirming an interpretation, namely, a thesis), this content can be none other than the sheer *thatness* of things: we realize that things are, that we are affected by them, and that we are always doing something about and with them, by intention or by default, rightly or wrongly. In contrast to the complexity of meanings, their content is revealed as a sustaining simplicity.

The answer to the original question is: Literature is a conflictive opening. It is evident, however, that this is a provisional answer and will be acceptable only to those who are willing to make, as Mallarmé does, a two-fold assumption: that for the most part we are closed off by our own devices from the content hidden away in things, and that this content is not another meaning of the things, but an emergence of the things themselves, in art.

IV

Literary interpretation is reflective articulation of the opening evoked by the work under consideration. It is successful in so far as it enhances our participation in the actual event of the work. To contribute to the work itself, it must above all preserve the original poetic articulation as it opens out upon its own content. Criticism at its best then has a poetic aspect, albeit one borrowed from the literature it interprets. But it is also reflective: it must restate the way in which the original is an opening. A poem, a novel, or a play cannot both open out upon content and state the means by which it does so, since all statements it does make contribute to the opening itself and dissolve in its favor.

The particular kind of interpretation which we here endorse —and try to exemplify—differs in one essential aspect from all others. Interpretation in the usual sense is assumed to aim at eliciting a special meaning or a manifold of meanings. Ordinarily one assumes that the work, the author, or the world itself contains, besides all the obvious and hackneyed meanings, an underlying set of meanings. It then becomes the task of the reflective mind with its tools to penetrate below the surface and to incorporate the special meanings of the work in its own discourse. However, it will be noticed that our own understanding of the nature of literature precludes the ultimate relevance of interpretation in the usual sense. The aim is not to get at underlying meanings. The aim is rather to articulate the available meanings so that they open out upon a content which is not itself another meaning, but the sheer simplicity and otherness of things sustaining human confortation with them. In our everyday life we may interpret the gestures of our host to mean that he is tired and would like us to go home so that he could go to bed. But when we "interpret" literature we restate all such meanings with a view to preserving their opening. This is a different and a rather special kind of interpretation, and so it deserves another name but one honored by time: we propose to call it *hermeneutics.*[6]

As a hybrid literature, literary criticism will come out of our understanding of the original literature which we are to interpret. If one understands the task of criticism to be the explicating of the meanings and inclinations initially harbored by the author, it is because one understands literature to be the exfoliation of a personality. If one understands the task to be the relating of the work to its age, it is because one understands literature to be the reflection of society at a particular stage of history. If one understands the task to be the extracting of a thesis regarding the nature of things, it is because one understands literature to be a vehicle of persuasion, an instrument of enlightment and/or an instigation to action. If one understands the task to be the defining of the style, it is because one understands literature to provide a system of fine and refined perceptions, and thereby an opportunity for the reader to develop his sensitivity to what goes on in human experience.

We shall not quarrel with the variety of conceptions about literary interpretation. Literature no doubt does often bring a personality to the fore, draw upon historical circumstances, convince us of the importance of one thing or another, and sharpen our perceptions. Different interpretations can underscore these various meanings. They can all contribute to a participation in the work itself—by emphasizing the materials and meanings which surrounded the production of the work—but they do not articulate the opening of the work. Hermeneutics does what other interpretations cannot do: it lets the literature do its own work. Hermeneutics articulates the opening in which these meanings become relevant and receive their ultimate justification. For the personal, social theoretical, and perceptive meanings found in literary works can be much more effectively carried out through other disciplines. Hegel assumed that the prime function of the arts and of literature was to present meanings (primarily those of religion). Since, according to Hegel, the human capacity to articulate meanings had developed to a higher level, he correctly said that meanings could be better presented elsewhere than in art. In that sense then art was for him something of the past. But in undertaking the hermeneutical approach to literature, we refrain from Hegel's assumption, and we allow literature to be of the present.

Hermeneutical literary criticism is an historical act. It brings the calcified meanings of the past to open out upon their content and so to configure into a present. We read a piece of fifty years ago or more, say, one by Proust: we witness personal sentiments and problems within a social and historical milieu. Until we achieve a certain level of "culture," we find Proust difficult. The meanings are rapidly closing themselves off from us. True, readers of the author's own time did not find his works very accessible. The reason for the difficulty is now different, though. From being totally strange and unfamiliar, the meanings articulated in Proust have now become all too familiar: precisely the "culture" necessary to read Proust equips us with ready-made interpretations of the significance of each of his meanings. We are familiar with the "accepted" interpretations of subjectivity, society, time, and perception, re-enforced now by the theories of psychoanalysis and of philosophy. These meanings hover in the air quite independently of the work in question, and the work seems to be a mere extension of these free-floating interpretations. Proust's novel is not a literary work in which we participate, but a fact which is tucked away in our culture. It lies there, dormant, until it is revived—almost as though by a miracle. Periodically we pull it out for inspection, its meanings undergo reclassification in a literature class. At a given moment it might even capture the odd student who, in spite of the "culture" surrounding it, might manage to recognize the opening it provides. In these rare and spontaneous cases, the hitherto calcified meanings are loosened up and brought to converge on the present. The historical act does not trace relations back into history; it allows these relations to construct, rather than obstruct, the present.

What defines hermeneutics as a historical act, then, is not the effort to ferret out the additional meanings surrounding the work in the milieu of its birth. Hermeneutics is an historical act because it attempts to dissolve the capacity of those meanings already embedded in the work so that they can truly converge upon the present and reveal it in the opening configured by them. Hermeneutics does not leave these meanings hovering vaguely on the horizon where they conceal from our view their actual content by always referring back to our pre-established ideas.

Our tradition of scholarship and learning demands that our research further knowledge and culminate in concrete results. The hermeneutical approach is aware of the dangers in this tradition. Let us listen, therefore, once again to Mallarmé who suggests the essence of interpretation in an image:

> In the poet's opinion, those individuals are wrong whose avowed project is to scoop out of some nightless inkwell the vain foundation sufficing for intelligibility. They act with little delicacy in giving the Crowd (including the Genius) such an access, allowing the vast incomprehension of mankind to pour out in a great din and racket. . . . Their enterprise is one of exhibiting things at their first level, where they have no power to perturb, just as newsboys do. . . . Rather than preserving the precious mist floating above the intimate abyss of each thought, they write in any given case with no justification except to spread banality abroad: for that is vulgar in which we can discern, just below the surface, the character of immediacy. . . . In place of the labyrinth illuminated by flowers and beckoning to leisure, these fellows, forever repeating the same thing, copy, upon a road lined with headaches, the resurrection of infinite blindness in vertical plaster casts, with no sheltered fountains nor any emergent greenery, but only the butts of bottles and awkward fragments. (M, 383-84)

This image is partly negative. However, the positive point is the sustaining one: To preserve the precious mist floating above the intimate abyss, the labyrinth illuminated by flowers and beckoning to leisure, we must care less for what we may carry away as our own than for what we may experience in the works themselves.

baudelaire and the modern age

Homer's account of Hephaistos, the blacksmith, in the *Iliad* (XVIII) portrays "man the maker," *homo faber,* in a paradoxical light revealing, as his story proceeds, the problematic character of Western man. In the same passage we experience the emergence of Achilles' shield in all its magnificence from the hand of the blacksmith, and we see Hephaistos a panting colossus bathed in sweat, burly breasted, stocky necked, and limping. The beautiful and the ugly side by side, the one brought out more clearly by its contrast with the other: on the one hand, a creation containing within itself a manifold of meanings for man; on the other hand, a process negating itself for the sake of an end lying outside itself—and in between these two a creativity sung by the poet himself in the course of his depiction. The tension strikes us as integrating these contrasting elements through the agency of art.

In the last hundred years or so the tension between creation and fabrication has taken a new form. We all recognize in the scientific revolution, the industrial revolution, and with the advent of technology, that there hangs over us a new form of relationship between doing and perceiving, making and conceiving, fabricating and creating. But what is most evident is that we are in the midst of something which we do not yet really understand but which nonetheless holds us in its sway. Meanwhile, we seek out some inevitably unhappy compromise. Either we tend to engage in hasty dealings to determine natural phenomena, to achieve financial solvency, and, at the summit, to master the entire cosmos in both its social and natural aspects. Or we tend to plunge into the soul-searching which seems necessary to come to terms with our own position within these dealings. The machine seems to need a ghost, but the ghost cannot quite make itself at home in the machine.

The twentieth century is only the continuation—or, if you wish, the maturation—of a rifted prodigality which became evident for the first time in sharp outline during the nineteenth century. It was then that the unresolved tension between creation and fabrication truly came to the fore in the form of a blind faith in the ability of man to turn things to his own use rather than to find himself and things in a reciprocal relationship. Among those who saw the significance and danger in what was happening, thereby seeing beyond the simple events, were the poets, and foremost among the poets is the figure of Baudelaire. We can catch a glimpse of a more germinal form of our contemporary experience of the rift by considering the testimony of this one man. For Baudelaire is both poet and critic, both one who strives to resolve the tension between creation and fabrication aesthetically and one who articulates the elements and the means of the resolution problematically. As for us, who probably cannot be both but must be content with being critics, we should keep a sharp eye out for any clue to understand what criticism might do and might contribute toward the needed resolution.

Let us begin with a review of Baudelaire's own perceptions about the problem as he experienced it. In his critique of Théophile Gautier dating from 1859, he gently admonishes the poet for his attempt to compromise with Industry and Progress, which Baudelaire capitalizes in the text, adding the qualifying phrase, "these despotic enemies of all poetry" (B, 700). In his effort to make his peace with everybody, Gautier had affirmed the contemporary upsurge of what for us is a more settled fact. Baudelaire takes exception to this act of benevolence. In his *Salon* of that same year and in his *Journaux intimes* of about the same time, we find a recurring concern for understanding the relationship between art and poetry, on the one hand, and progress and industry, now called more simply technology, on the other.

It is not an easy matter to achieve a clear idea of what we mean by progress. Baudelaire offers a rather neutral definition and commentary of it in a criticism entitled *Exposition Universelle* (1855). In the section "Method of Criticism," subtitled "On the Modern Idea of Progress Applied to the Fine Arts: Displacement of Vitality," he mentions several examples of progress: 1) the case of a nation coming to understand moral questions more subtly, 2) the case of an artist producing a work which testifies to more knowledge and imaginative force than his previous work did; and 3) the case of marketable commodities becoming of better quality and selling better than they had the day before. With these concrete examples in mind, Baudelaire asks: What guarantees that any instance of progress will continue tomorrow? The question is justified. While examples of progress can only be drawn from comparisons between the past and the present, anybody who thinks seriously about progress, understands it as an infinite series extending into the future. Thus, any belief that the progress of yesterday and today will continue into the morrow is located in one's own blind faith and conceit. In other words, although progress is indeed something which occurs, it is itself a dream when it is taken out of its function as a category of comparison between the past and the present and elevated to the status of ensuring goals for the future. Ordinarily, however, such elevation is not accepted in the status of a dream but in the status of a truth. This discrepancy gives rise to Baudelaire's thought that, after all, "infinite progress might be humanity's most ingenious and cruel torture." For nobody knows (B, 958-59).

If we ask Baudelaire, as we must, why progress can pose a dangerous problem as well as mark a desirable development, we receive in reply what at first appears to be the usual answer, and one that is not very enlightening because of its familiarity. In a parenthetical remark Baudelaire gives a moral, as contrasted to a formal and neutral, definition of progress: "I understand by progress the progressive diminution of the soul and the progressive domination of matter" (B, 1032-33). In a moral context the word "soul" refers here to the depth of experience and the truthfulness—the true nature—of man, and the word "matter" refers to the surface of experience and the spuriousness—the spurious aspects—of man. Progress is a fact, as a consideration of Baudelaire's concrete examples cannot but lead us to admit. Not all facts, however, can serve as ideals for man. The case of progress is merely such a case. Progress is itself an outer manifestation, an aftereffect, really an afterfact. To transmute it into an ideal makes the future only an imitation of the past—and so, paradoxial as it indeed seems, it amounts to a denial of the future. It gives us momentary and even deserved pleasure to witness a more subtle understanding of moral questions, a more penetrating knowledge and imaginative force in our creations, more satisfactory commodities on a better market. But if we then idolized the progress which we note, we grasp at the shadow rather than at the substance—and eventually lose sight of both, sinking into nihilism. And yet the life of man, as evidenced in the history both of the individual and of the race, seems to be well sketched out as the development of increasing tension between substance and shadow, between the penetration of human insight and the aftereffects of human prowess. Speaking at a time when this tension was first showing signs of breaking the spirit of man rather than propelling him on, Baudelaire remarks apocalyptically: "Mechanics will have Americanized us so much, progress will have atrophied the spiritual part of us to such an extent, that nothing among the bloody, sacrilegious or antinatural dreams of the uto- pians will be comparable to its concrete results" (B, 1263).

It is the same with industry. What impresses Baudelaire is not so much the advent of large factories, mass labor, and the con- comitant transformation of rural into urban life, but the character of human ambition which becomes prominent and seemingly justi- fied throughout these more obvious events. In industry human am- bition becomes devoted to clear-headedness, explicitness, clarity. It is the mark of this kind of devotion that there arises within it a perspicuous relationship with the rude facts and circumstances of life. It is noteworthy that Baudelaire considers photography to be a very effective example of industry: *we* would probably conjure up an image of some block-long factory situated in the impoverished outskirts of town, complete with a clear-sighted manager and a host of efficient clerks to keep track of the workers beyond the air-con- ditioned rooms. In either case, however, Baudelaire sees the same ambition: a careful and exact perception of facts, a perception suf- ficient unto itself, independent of prior history or future ideals— or at least apparently so.

We ask what could possibly be wrong with clear-headedness and perspicuity. The answer can only be: nothing. A man of poetic interests could hardly do without an unusually high degree of pre- cisely these virtues. But danger lurks in any virtue. A virtue is what it is only within a certain context of interests and so may transform itself into a vice upon being transferred to another domain. The question we must ask, then, is not what is wrong with this character of industry, but what is *dangerous* about it, and why. With this relocation of the question, we can see Baudelaire giving a clear reply. In some notes intended for his work, *"Mon Coeur mis à nu,"* which was never completed, he discusses the subject of industry in one of its more concrete and specific forms, namely, that of commercial enterprise. Baudelaire is much impressed by this phenomenon of commerce, as his notes and letters on Belgium testify more fully (B, 1371). "Commerce is, by its very essence, *satanic,"* he says (B, 1297). For Baudelaire commerce incarnates an ambition and devotion in which getting outdistances giving. In industry and commerce we have not just isolated instances but rather the general embodiment and apparent justification for man to reduce the world to the status of self-perpetuating material. When Baudelaire goes on to say: "Commerce is satanic because it is a form of egotism, the lowest and vilest," we must keep in mind the reason for his condemnation and see its ever more subtle implications. Egotism here hardly consists in perceiving the world as material for one's own spiritual construction, since this kind of perceiving might very well be that of the poet. Rather, it consists in abstracting only the moment of perceiving material and justifying this abstraction in term of further materials. What makes egotism base and vile is that precisely by reducing the activity of the ego to the acute but exclusive perception of material, the ego is defaced and debilitated. Baudelaire sees in this abstraction and reduction a socio-historical confirmation and encouragement of the natural state of affairs—that natural state which man needs above all to transform and transcend: "Commerce is *natural, therefore* it is *infamous"* (ibid).

Technology as we know it today is actually the progeny of an apparently happy marriage between the ideals of scientific progress and commercial industry. An euphoric child, it embodies the more viable and tones down the more self-defeating characteristics of its two parents. Technology is an attitude which directs us toward the futural and the new; but it also instills in us the thought that the movement into the future is one of our own making rather than one of qualifying the natural course of events as such. Technology is furthermore an attitude which directs us to the continual satiation of material interests, but which understands that this process can only realize itself on the condition that we renounce specific "selfish" forms of satiation and concentrate upon the general "humanistic" forms. Technology is a way of life, the form in which we experience the world today; it is not just one thing among others to be found in the contemporary catalogue of the paths of men. In this respect we live in a different era than did Baudelaire: today everything we do or experience takes its shape in the light and dark of this amalgam, whether we are in pursuit of it or in flight from it.

We ask again what could possibly be dangerous about this progeny considered in its own nature. Only now we must ask what the relevance of such consideration might be for the contemporary understanding of art, poetry, and criticism.

We find a clue in Baudelaire's timely, simple, and pointed remarks about the rise of photography found in the section of the *Salon de 1859* entitled "The Modern Public and Photography" (B, 1031-36). Photography may well have given up the kind of aspirations it had at the time of its first appearance, for it is now something of an art itself. But at our first exposure to it we all probably experience a sentiment very much akin to what our forefathers felt: the apparent claim of a photograph is to depict what simply *is*, already is, apart from human interests and prejudice. Baudelaire recognizes the naïveté of this claim in two ways. First, a photograph captures its subjects only by a process of selection governed by certain human interests which it ultimately portrays; only fools (*insensés*) can believe that exactitude is possible in abstraction. But Baudelaire prefers to dwell upon a second abstraction in photography, one perhaps possible and yet ultimately fatal for man. "The exclusive taste for the true," Baudelaire says, " . . . here oppresses and suffocates the taste for the beautiful" (B, 1033). He sees in photography the rise of an ideal working against art, namely, the ideal of perceiving things exactly the way they are, that is, the way they present themselves apart from any modification of their countenance through human involvement with them. Art, according to Baudelaire, is the process of recreating things in and through a special activity. In art human interests are inserted into the experience of things in such a way that the interest weds itself to the things and thereby modifies their countenance. For Baudelaire photography is a satanic competitor or opponent for art, since a photograph can do little, if anything, to enforce the modification of the appearance of things through the integration of human interests within the experience of them. In the same context he remarks: "Poetry and progress are two ambitions which hate each other with an instinctive hatred, and whenever they meet on the same road one of the two inevitably has to serve the other" (B. 1035).

At first sight we might be tempted to generalize Baudelaire's thought and set it into a contemporary vein by saying that, as far as he is concerned, technology is an abstract attitude and drive for truth and, as such, should be subordinated to the ideal of art. But let us not be misguided, for if we undertake a superficial reading of Baudelaire's words here, we do an injustice both to him and to the various phenomena of the world such as photography and art. Let us therefore hazard another paraphrase of Baudelaire's meaning. What has to be discerned as never before is both the difference and the relationship between the perception and the consummation of materials in art and life. The various historical developments which fall under the heading of progress and industry, or today under technology, tend more and more to confirm and encourage an abstract movement of man toward clarity about materials *apart from* the fulfillment of the experience in which such clarity becomes truly relevant. In Baudelaire's terms, we assume erroneously that if we perceive enough truths about the way things naturally are, we will be naturally propelled into the experience of beauty and the fulfillment of experience. This assumption sums up the nineteenth-century naïveté of which Baudelaire was keenly aware— and suggests the location of the twentieth-century disillusionment which we are presently beginning to experience in its fullest thrust. This assumption not only works against art, it works against man.

For Baudelaire, consummation or fulfillment of human experience is art. In his critique of Théophile Gautier he says: "Poetry . . . has no other end but Itself; it cannot have another..." (B, 685). And in the *Salon de 1846* he writes: "You can live three days without bread;—without poetry, not at all; and those among you who say the opposite are deceived: you do not know yourselves" (B, 874). From these and similar passages, we can see that whenever Baudelaire thinks and speaks of art or poetry he is thinking and speaking of a form of consummation which belongs to man as such, to human experience as such. What is most important for man — what sustains us in whatever we do and whoever we are — is the experience of, or participation in, what has only itself as its end or purpose. And it is this which, by Baudelaire's definition, art and poetry provide.

Technology, by its very nature, cannot provide, and rather resists, the experience of consummation. We say by its very nature, because technology as our historical mode of living and thinking is precisely the aggrandizement of extrinsic perception, the constant encouragement to take one thing only for an end beyond that thing, an end which in turn gets subsumed under a further end, and so on. In other words, the reign of technology is the reign of the perception of materials, of means, and this reign brings with it the claim that technology itself does not stand in need of anything beyond itself. This self-contradictory claim belonging to the very nature of technology amounts to a claim to be art. In a mock formulation of the thoughts of his own contemporary enthusiasts, Baudelaire says: "Because photography provides all the desirable guarantees of exactitude (they believe that, the fools!), art is photography" (B, 1034).

But now is the time for a double take. When we first analyze the structure and meaning of technology, we are struck by its being a way of experiencing material. However, the decisive moment in history is arriving when we must see that technology is "material" in another way. Notwithstanding its apparent claim to self-sufficiency, it is in itself and as a totality material for a higher purpose. It is, namely, the material character of our experience, the material which the poet and artist recreates for himself, for his time, and for his posterity. At one time the city-state, as it was fated by the gods, was material for art; at another time the church, as it was the mediator of man's relation to the one God, was material for art; at still another time the aristocracy, as it personified human perfection, was material for art; and now for over one hundred years progress, industry, and technology are material, presumably once again, for art. Creativity is most basically exercised in the face of such materials and those materials always make a claim to self-sufficiency, thereby resisting the work of the poet and artist. Meeting this claim and resisting it are at least part of the challenge.

Baudelaire's own creativity provides an example of what technology can mean for art and poetry today. In spite of all he says against progress and industry in his essays, his poetry is distinctively urban. His works sing of the city, precisely the location of progress, industry, and the advent of technology. Evidently the poet's dissatisfaction with modern trends is no mere yearning for a return to the quiet life of the pre-industrial age. Rather, it is an expression of a profound realization that the phenomena of modern urban life have to be absorbed into a poetic mode of experience. Poetry and art celebrate what we otherwise experience as flat. If what we now experience is urban, and if urban phenomena are in themselves flat, then the task of the poet is to celebrate urban phenomena—not as they simply appear, of course, but as they reappear in poetic works.

Let us take Baudelaire's *"Le Crépuscule du matin"* as an example of a poetic re-articulation of urban phenomena. The poem is found in *"Scènes parisiennes"* of *Les Fleurs du mal* (B, 99). The poetic quality of the original is enhanced by the Alexandrian verse and classical rhyme.

LE CRÉPUSCULE DU MATIN

La diane chantait dans les cours des casernes,
Et le vent du matin soufflait sur les lanternes.

C'était l'heure où l'essaim des rêves malfaisants
Tord sur leurs oreillers les bruns adolescents;
Où comme un oeil sanglant qui palpite et qui bouge,
La lampe sur le jour fait une tâche rouge;
Où l'âme, sous le poids du corps revêche et lourd,
Imite les combats de la lampe et du jour.
Comme un visage en pleurs que les brises essuient,
L'air est plein du frisson des choses qui s'enfuient,
Et l'homme est las d'écrire et la femme d'aimer.

Les maisons çà et là commençaient à fumer.
Les femmes de plaisir, la paupière livide,
Bouche ouverte, dormaient de leur sommeil stupide;
Les pauvresses, traînant leurs seins maigres et froids,
Soufflaient sur leurs tisons et soufflaient sur leurs doigts.
C'était l'heure où parmi le froid et la lésine
S'aggravent les douleurs des femmes en gésine;
Comme un sanglot coupé par un sang écumeux
Le chant du coq au loin déchirait l'air brumeux;
Une mer de brouillards baignait les édifices,
Et les agonisants dans le fond des hospices

Poussaient leur dernier râle en hoquets inégaux.
Poussaient leur dernier râle en hoquets inégaux.

L'aurore grelottante en robe rose et verte
S'avançait lentement sur la Seine déserte,
Et le sombre Paris, en se frottant les yeux,
Empoignait ses outils, vieillard laborieux.

MORNING TWILIGHT

Reveille was sounding into the barrack squares,
And the morning wind was blowing onto the street
    lamps.

It was that hour when swarms of maleficent dreams
Twist brown adolescents upon their pillows;
When, like a bloodshot eye which quakes and cringes,
The lamp makes a red spot onto the day;
When the soul, beneath the body's churlish and
    imposing weight,
Imitates the struggles of the lamp and day.
Like a face in tears wiped by the breeze,
The air is filled with the shivers of things which flee,
And man is tired of writing, and woman of loving.

Here and there the houses were beginning to smoke.
Women of the street, with livid eyelids,
Open-mouthed, were sunk into stupid sleep.
And women papers, dragging their meager and
    chilled breasts,
Were blowing on their embers and on their fingers.
It was that hour when, amidst the cold and misery,
Women's labor pains increase.
Like a sob broken by a foamy jet of blood
The cry of a distant cock was slitting the fogged air.
A sea of mist was bathing the buildings,
And from the interior of hospitals, the dying
Were emitting their last breath in convulsive rattles.

ERRATA

p. 38, 2nd line: delete whole line and insert *Les débauchés rentraient, brisés par leurs travaux.*

p. 38, 4th line of third English stanza: for *papers* read *paupers*

p. 53, 3rd line of 3rd English paragraph: read *voluptuousness*

p. 93, 1st line of French poem: read *rencontrée*

p. 93, 2nd line of French poem: read *toujours*

p. 98, 1st line: for *Sound* read *Sounds*

p. 118, last line: read *l'héroïsme*

p. 119, 7th line of 2nd English stanza: read *diluvian*

P. 119, 6th line of 3rd English stanza: read *illuminating*

> *Debauched revelers were coming in, broken by their
> labors.*
>
> *Dawn, shuddering in her rose and green dress,*
> *Was slowly advancing on the deserted river Seine,*
> *And somber Paris, rubbing its eyes,*
> *Was taking up its tools, an agèd toiler.*

The opening stanza sets the scene in most vivid terms. We look in upon barracks, presumably military barracks. It is early morning, for reveille is being sounded. And the brisk morning wind blows onto what man has constructed in an effort to counter the forces of night—not onto man, but onto the artifacts of man, the street lamps. The scene is set in the imperfect tense; what we are looking in upon is neither simply present nor simply past, it is established.

> *Reveille was sounding into the barrack squares,*
> *And the morning wind was blowing onto the street lamps.*

In just two verses, in two brush strokes, a poetic space is stretching out before us. We are transported into a particular world: neither that of nature (country-side, mountain peaks, stormy seas), nor that of the gods (powers of creation, powers of destiny), but rather the world of human prowess as suggested by the harshest of human architecture (barracks) and the most unending of human efforts (the supplying of light to counteract darkness)—with just a hint of human and natural life (the reveille and the wind). This space is set "in time": it is neither a futural possibility, nor a present circumstance unfolding before us, nor a past and gone happening: it is neither hope, fact, nor history. The space is experienced in the mode of unfolding as this unfolding is as a whole established. The remaining stanzas of the poem necessitate this peculiar temporal qualification. For the matinal space of the poem is one in which we experience things not so much waking up as dying away. In a companion poem, *"Le Crépuscule du soir"* earlier in same section of *Les Fleurs du mal* (B, 90), the space of evening is a time of awakening, a *present* unfolding where one has to brace oneself for what is coming. Every space must have its time.

The poem as a whole retains its space. It must do so if it is to provide for celebrative and poetic experience. The commonest utterance depends upon a space for its intelligibility, since it issues from a particular world and makes sense to others as they are turned toward its framework. Ordinarily, when someone talks about reveille and barracks, wind and street lamps, we accept the relevant context of space and time according to some course of practical concern. For instance, a soldier hears in the reveille the need to rise and in the wind the need to dress in a fitting manner. The soldier would not ordinarily fix his attention on the temporal and spatial context as a whole, since his attention is naturally drawn to and from the things within the context. If the soldier enjoys recounting his experiences in his old age, or listening in the evening to accounts of actual or imaginary events relating to military life, his enjoyment is no doubt artistic in part. He is then seeking the sustenance of his particular world in the retention of its space, something which can happen in an elementary fashion through re-articulation. An articulation that retains its space integrates comments which deliberately or intentionally deviate from our usual, distracting practical concerns, from those concerns which obliterate the space itself. To speak of the morning wind as blowing onto the street lamps, for example, is to focus on events related in themselves to one another quite indifferently to immediate human concerns. If the poet had said instead that the wind was blowing in through the windows, the poetic space would have been weakened if not lost.

Some poems simply state a space and allow things to emerge within it to invade our attention and provide a momentary aesthetic delight. Consider, for instance, the English translation of the Chinese poem by T'ao Ch'ien:

NEW CORN

Swiftly the years, beyond recall.
Solemn the stillness of this fair morning.
I will clothe myself in spring clothing
And visit the slopes of the Eastern Hill.
By the mountain stream a mist hovers,
Hovers a moment, then scatters.

> *There comes a wind blowing from the south*
> *That brushes the fields of new corn.*[16]

In this poem the first verse provides a temporal qualification, akin to the imperfect tense, for the space configured in the following verses. Morning, human action, natural phenomena, wind and corn (a *natural* product of *human* effort) are then articulated into a space from which practical concerns are purged for the sake of an experience of things as they simply are, i.e., as they simply emerge within the space.

In Baudelaire's poem, however, the initial space is subsequently retained by and filled out with an overwhelming multitude of images drawn from the sordid, obvious, and definitive side of urban life. The space initially formed is thus given greater definition than the space formed by the Chinese poem. The experience of *"Le Crépuscule du matin"* brings us face to face with natural and man-made things, and also with a defined mode of human response to them. In the first stanza of this poem and the whole of the Chinese poem, not only are the things told but also told is the way these things are to be experienced.

The second stanza of *"Le Crépuscule"* articulates a multitude of typical images of that hour of morning twilight. "It was the hour when . . . ," and what follows is a series of rapidly redirected and refocusing perceptions: from the maleficent dreams of youths, to a quaking, cringing, bloodshot eye, to the human soul which, as the lamp and the day, struggles with the body, to tears and to the breeze, and, in the last verse, to the exhaustions incurred by writing and loving. The poetic space is being filled with a plenitude of things and people. It is furthermore given a very definite mood as well. Morning time is a time of beginning; for many it is a time of energy, of hope, of willingness to confront things as they come; for others it is a time to discern once again the dawn of creation or the awakening of nature in the growing light and singing birds. However, the stanza intentionally violates the mood of beginning. Although the hour is one of emergence, there is a marked unwillingness on the part of human beings to rise to this emergence. The mood is one of conflict. Maleficent dreams rather than sustaining hopes occupy the minds of youth. The body resists the soul, man-made light battles with nature-made light. The penultimate verse,

The air is filled with the shivers of things which flee,

epitomizes the conflict. Contrary to what one might presume, things are not coming out for what they are at this moment of morning twilight. They are withdrawing, lapsing into nothingness. The last verse of the stanza,

And man is tired of writing, and woman of loving,

captures a furtive image of man and woman, the one as active and the other as receptive, both as having arrived at the nadir of their being. This very carefully presented series of conflicting and balancing images instills into the poetic space of the poem a mood which itself conflicts with our own immediate disposition toward the morning, the disposition to find zest in life.

The mood remains one of emergence, the dismalness of the poetic space notwithstanding. There is no suggestion that we who are experiencing this space are to turn away from what continues to arise in it, to yearn for the return of the same night, or to look forward to the coming of the next day. Introducing a definite mood into a poetic space is a most delicate operation: the space may be dissolved or enhanced, all according to whether we are drawn away from or on toward what is depicted within the space. In "*Le Crépuscule du matin*" the poet has avoided the obvious pitfalls. Baudelaire's success in this regard is impressive indeed, for throughout the bulk of his work he definitely favors night-time over daytime. "*Le Crépuscule du soir*" is in one respect much more easily executed, since for the evening the poet can more easily provide a space-enhancing mood, when things are looming rather than withdrawing, when we can meet them halfway and do not have to pursue them all the way, as in "*Le Crépuscule du matin.*" In passing, we can note Baudelaire's own formulation of the artist's nighttime enterprise in his essay "*Le Peintre de la vie moderne*" (B, 1162):

> Now, at the hour when others are sleeping, he [the one gifted with the faculty of seeing, and possessing the power of expressing] is bent over his table, casting onto a sheet of paper the same look which, just a while ago, he was attaching to things, juggling with his pencil, his pen, his brush, making the water in his

glass leap to the ceiling, wiping his pen on his shirt, rushed, violent, active, as though he were afraid the images would run away from him, a quarreler even when alone, hurrying himself along. And the things are reborn on paper. . . .

Although no doubt written at night and in the mood described by Baudelaire, *"Le Crépuscule du matin"* directs our attention to the things of the day.

We are asked to experience things in the morning in a way suitable for the nature of city life. Street lamps and sidewalks, shops and factories have no life of their own. Unlike things in nature, urban phenomena show no vitality until the human spirit is once again instilled into them. In the city, we are indeed at "point zero" each morning, and each dawn requires that we re-instill vitality into the otherwise empty shells of urban life. In the country we wake up fresh and ready to meet the oncoming day; in the city we drag ourselves out of bed and reluctantly prepare ourselves to race after the day. It is because the second stanza places us in the mood of "point zero" that the poetic space of the poem is urban in character. Otherwise, only the general title of the group of poems, *"Tableaux Parisiens,"* and the penultimate verse of the last stanza, would inform us of the urban setting. The power of the second stanza shows that we do not need this information. The second stanza bolsters the aesthetic space and orients us toward the content of this space in such a way that prominent epochal meanings are incorporated into the process of perception.

The third stanza, the longest of the four, fills in the space defining our perception. In contrast with the previous stanza, the particular comes forth here; the general and the metaphorical are subdued:

Here and there the houses were beginning to smoke.

This verse brings into focus the first sign of a possible vitality. Smoke winding from the chimney into the morning air evokes directly the initial efforts of men and women to rise to the day. But as the remaining twelve verses of this stanza take us into the houses and before the hearth, we are again placed at "point zero." Rather than witnessing people absentmindedly preparing for another day's work, we see prostitutes at the end of their rope, paupers managing as best they can, the increasing pain of childbirth, a cock crowing indifferently through the fog, moribund patients in the hospital, and, finally, debauched revelers who, like the prostitutes, are also at the end of their rope. The poet's selection of particular images here conforms with his statement of general images in the first stanza: the stupidity of evil and the pain of poverty, the pain of death and the exhaustion of debauchery. Dawn in the city is not defined by a bright and cheery sun recalling things to their natural vitality, nor is it marked by cheerfully disposed men and women who are recalled from the night.

In the prefatory dedication to the volume of his prose poems *Spleen de Paris*, Baudelaire suggests the relevance of his choice of negative images (B, 229).

> Who among us has not dreamed, in his more ambitious days, of the miracle of a poetic prose, musical and yet without either rhythm or rhyme, supple and jostled enough to adapt itself to the lyrical movements of the soul, to the undulations of reverie, to the palpitations of conscious life?

> It is above all when we frequent the large cities, it is from the crisscrossing of their innumerable interrelations, that this obsessive ideal is born.

By filling the poetic space with sordid rather than cheery elements, the poet is emphasizing the human role in the moment of emergence, in the matinal emergence of the poem. If in urban life man must each day revitalize his circumstances, each day he will then again experience the nadir of his own being and the nothingness of things. Point zero calls attention to man, and the poem evokes his "lyrical movements"—not, we notice, to glorify man but rather to reveal what man has to face. "*Le Crépuscule du matin*" is hardly a romantic depiction of the human soul: it is through the movements, undulations, and palpitations of man that the city itself, at its moment of emergence, is seen and momentarily held in view.

The air of simplicity introduced by the fourth and final stanza seals the poetic space and terminates our search for further content within it:

Dawn shuddering in her rose and green dress
Was slowly advancing upon the deserted river Seine,
And somber Paris, rubbing its eyes,
Was taking up its tools, an agèd toiler.

Dawn and the river are both natural phenomena; the one is out of sorts and the other is deserted. Paris, on the other hand, is a totality of urban phenomena. And it is this totality that has been waking up and taking up its tools. The city itself, and as a whole, is presented as an "agèd toiler." Such is the character of urban life that its vitality waxes and wanes as a whole, as its intricate, complex, and overwhelming machinery is set in motion early each day and shut down late each night.

These final verses add a prospective stance. The previous images have thrust our attention back upon the night. With evident intention the last stanza prevents us from doting on the past by opening us out to the impending future, the day itself: Paris takes up its tools. If we start with the sordid elements and conflict-ridden moods in this poem, it is not because we are to dwell upon such things lethargically, sentimentally, or individually: it is because that is where we start, and we only start when we move on, "an agèd toiler."

No doubt the purport of *"Le Crépuscule du matin"* is negative in part. Most poems in *Les Fleurs du mal* attempt to articulate evil aesthetically. An image which compares the struggle of dawn and street lamps to the twitching of a bloody eye is meant to shock us, to estrange us from the familiar world, to prevent us from responding to the subject matter of the poem, morning twilight, in our habitual and oblivious manner. But the task of articulating these otherwise negative elements aesthetically is fulfilled only when they are transformed into the new, the revitalized, the positive. This Baudelaire does by describing the sordid elements in such a way that they can reappear as a beginning, here the beginning of the day, and so an emergence of content for man. In spite of all the evil depicted in the poem, evil both incurred by and inflicted upon men and women, a tone of serene acceptance runs through the verses and climaxes in the last stanza. The acceptance is neither sordid itself nor is it resigned. Neither the human implication in evil nor the inevitability of painful circumstances is accepted. What is accepted is the task of beginning at point zero, confronting things as they indeed are at that point, and working from there.

The passage quoted earlier from *"Le Peintre de la vie moderne,"* describing how the artist works at night, continues:

> . . . And the things are reborn on paper, natural and more than natural, beautiful and more than beautiful, singular and endowed with an enthusiastic life such as is the soul of the author. The phantasmagoria has been extracted from nature. All the materials with which the memory has encumbered itself get classified, ranked, harmonized; they submit to this forced idealization which is the result of *a childlike* perception, i.e., sharp perception, magical by virtue of its ingenuousness.

Things are "reborn on paper" because they have been revitalized into "enthusiastic life" according to the "soul of the author." Baudelaire does not say that this revitalization is achieved by the artist. The life of things reborn is not a mere projection of a subjectivity. Things that receive their life solely from such subjective projection remain as flat afterwards as they were at the outset. The men and women in the houses and on the streets, and the poet and artist contribute to the life of the city. However, they can not and do not consider themselves as the subjective source of its vitality. As individuals they stand each morning in the city at the nadir of their own being before the nothingness of things. Although they are held responsible for a rebirth of vitality, they are certainly powerless to proclaim it as of their own making.

"Le Crépuscule du matin" exemplifies how the poet may undertake the task of revitalizing urban phenomena. The poetic space of the poem discloses its sensuous content (particularly in the third stanza) correlative to the human forces constituting the mood articulated simultaneously with the content (particularly in the second stanza). The poet is calling upon two very different, though poetically related, kinds of materials: the sensuous and the historical. Things are reborn when both kinds of materials are incorporated into aesthetic articulation—not additively, but conflictively:

the historical forces of city life, of commerce, industry, and technology are brought to bear upon what presents itself at the moment. Particularly in urban morning hours, there is a gap and a conflict between the two. Accordingly "Le Crépuscule du matin" plays upon this reluctance to ensure the sense of emergence. As a result there is what Emmanuel Kant called a "free play of the presentative powers," that is, a liberating confrontation of our "power of taking in images" from sensation and our "understanding" which operates to unify an experience in concepts.[17] Hegel saw this liberation to be distinctively historical as well as logical and, specifically in our own time, Heidegger is describing the same liberation anew when he speaks of art work articulating a particular historical *world* of human aspirations as the self-concealing *earth* towers into that world in conflict *(Streit)*.[18] For Baudelaire the materials brought forward in memory not only get classified, ranked, and harmonized: in this organization they submit to what results from and so allows for *"childlike* perception," i.e., perception of what directly presents itself in all its singularity to man as artist.

Art embodies a conflict. To the extent that an art work incorporates into its space a precise, historically defined way of experiencing things, the conflict becomes critical. The Chinese poem "New Corn" simply forms its poetic space: we here experience things without being told specifically how they are to appear; its world is immediately transparent to things. In contrast, *"Le Crépuscule du matin"* achieves its transparency and vitality in a critical balance of conflictive materials. The art work is preserved and consummated only as we ourselves become critics, i.e., critical, careful. Criticism is critical and careful participation in the process of emergence (of things) and consummation (of experience). Art works incorporate much material of memory. As we participate in the space prepared for us by the poet or artist, we must be willing to allow such material to remain transparent to *"childlike* perception." Consummation of the historically given mode of our experience is the reward of such critical participation.

Baudelaire himself, one of the first poets to be a critic as well, remarked in "What Is the Purpose of Criticism?" a section of *Salon de 1846* "I sincerely believe that the best critique is one which is amusing and poetic, not one which is cold and algebraic and which, with the pretext of explaining everything, has neither hatred nor love, and voluntarily casts off every kind of mood" (B, 877). And again: "As for criticism properly so called, . . . I mean when I say that to be right, that is, to justify its own existence, criticism must be partial, passionate, political [in the French sense of having a purpose and aim]; it must be made from an exclusive point of view, but one which opens the most horizons" (B, 877). And finally: "As the arts always express the beautiful by a senti- ment, by the passion and reverie of each man—which amounts to saying that the arts are variety in unity of diverse countenances of the absolute—criticism touches upon metaphysics at every in- stant" (B, 878). These three passages, among the first commen- taries made by a poetic mind on the subject of criticism, say at least three things: Criticism is itself to take on a mood or temperament; that is, it is to do what creativity does and not take an outside view of it. It is to embody a particular stance rather than an uncommitted one; again, it is to do what creativity does. Finally, it is to capture the single issue underlying the manifold of appearances; it is to do not only what the poetic mind does but also something very akin to what the reflective mind does. In other words, we are asked to take part in the event of art and poetry rather than to convert it back into the status of some material in the world to be looked at or taken up into other designs.

Consummation is always consummation of what we exper- ience. What we experience, however, is the character of our ap- proach to things; in this sense, even the rudest of experiences refers us to the materials of the world in a kind of transcendence, and no experience can be one of simple sensation. What we experience today is technology. What we inevitably find in truly contemporary Western art is therefore a bringing to consummation of a material, technology, which quite naturally resists such treatment. What we as critics need to do is to participate in this movement and to aid each other, and anybody else interested, in entering into it also. Not that we conform to it, taking on its particular character, emu- lating its goals, and trying to share in its own kind of apparent glory. On the contrary. Rather than vainly attempting to participate in technology (we all participate in it whether we like it or not), we must creatively participate in the consummation of it; these are two different things. If the experience of art and poetry, as contrasted to that of progress and industry, is momentary, residing as it does in the momentary confrontation with and absorption in a poem, a play, a painting, a sculpture, so too might criticism take concrete form only as a fleeting embodiment of movement from material to consummation. If so, then criticism is both more sublime and more humble than we ordinarily suppose.

baudelaire and the experience of art

Charles Baudelaire has often been called the initiator of modern art and aesthetics, that is to say, of modern trends both in the various arts, such as painting and poetry, and in the conceptions and theories about them. Critics and poets—P. Valéry, T.S. Eliot, H.v. Hofmannsthal, H. Friedrich, M. Butor, M. Gilman, J. Maritain, to name but a few—claim that a new footing was achieved in and through the works of Baudelaire, and that this footing provided a legacy for further developments still in progress today. But this is easier said than understood. It is indeed easy enough to remark the striking differences in the literary and artistic world before and after the appearance of Baudelaire's works, but the enumeration of these differences never makes clear what it is *in* his works that possesses the tremendous power necessary to reroute the tradition. We will now consider the question: Wherein does this definitive power lie?

To answer this question the discussion will fall into two parts. The first interprets in some detail Baudelaire's prose poem *"Le Confiteor de l'artiste"* (B, 232) with a view to pointing out that the ambivalent experiences invoked and presented in the poem form the region where the fundamental possibilities of art loom up. The second will discuss how Baudelaire, in his *Curiosités esthétiques* and *L'Art romantique,* theoretically conceived the fundamental ground of artistic creation. Here we shall see that Baudelaire's aesthetic conceptions about the origin of the work of art and its status vis-à-vis reality are actually, that is, concretely and poetically, embodied in the ambivalent experiences peculiarly presented by the *"Confiteor."* Thus we will survey Baudelaire as both a poet and an aesthetician, and discover a certain accord between these two aspects of his works. Jacques Maritain asserts rightly that with Baudelaire "poetry became self-conscious" and that in this critical remove from subject matter hitherto unquestioned lies the beginning of the modern probe into the origin of the work of art. We shall discuss Baudelaire's modernity in terms of his three-fold belief that the work of art is a break with reality, that it is moreover a destruction of it, and that art stands self-sufficiently by itself, having, so to speak, a substance of its own apart from any service which it might seem to render outside of itself—being, in a word, an absolute.

LE CONFITEOR DE L'ARTISTE

Que les fins de journées d'automne sont pénétrantes! Ah! pénétrantes jusqu' à la douleur! car il est de certaines sensations délicieuses dont le vague n'exclut pas l'intensité; et il n'est pas de pointe plus acérée que celle de l'Infini.

Grand délice que celui de noyer son regard dans l'immensité du ciel et de la mer! Solitude, silence, incomparable chasteté de l'azur! une petite voile frissonnante à l'horizon, et qui par sa petitesse et son isolement imite mon irrémédiable existence, mélodie monotone de la houle, toutes ces choses pensent par moi, ou je pense par elles (car dans la grandeur de la rêverie, le moi se perd vite!); elles pensent, dis-je, mais musicalement et pittoresquement, sans arguties, sans syllogismes, sans déductions.

Toutefois, ces pensées, qu'elles sortent de moi ou s'élancent des choses, deviennent bientôt trop intenses. L'énergie dans la volupté crée un malaise et une souffrance positive. Mes nerfs trop tendus ne donnent plus que des vibrations criardes et douloureuses.

Et maintenant la profondeur du ciel me consterne; sa limpidité m'exaspère. L'insensibilité de la mer, l'immuabilité du spectacle me révoltent . . . Ah! faut-il éternellement souffrir, ou fuir éternellement le beau!

Nature, enchanteresse sans pitié, rivale toujours vic-
torieuse, laisse-moi! Cesse de tenter mes désirs et mon
orgueil! L'étude du beau est un duel où l'artiste crie
de frayeur avant d'être vaincu.

THE CONFITEOR OF THE ARTIST

How penetrating the ends of autumn days are! Ah!
penetrating to the point of pain! For there are certain
delicious sensations, the vagueness of which does not
exclude their intensity; and there is no jab sharper
than that of the Infinite.

A great delight it is to drown one's glance in the
immensity of the sky and the sea! Solitude, silence, in-
comparable chastity of the blue sky! a small quivering
sail at the horizon, which by its smallness and isolation
imitates my irremediable existence, monotonous mel-
ody of the surf, all these things think through me, or I
think through them (for in the greatness of reverie,
the self loses itself rapidly!); they think, I say, but
musically and picturesquely, without quibbles, with-
out syllogisms, without deductions.

But then these thoughts, whether they emerge from
me or spring from things, soon become too intense.
Energy within voluptuousness creates an uneasiness
and a positive suffering. My too tensed nerves emit
nothing but screaming and painful vibrations.

And now the depth of the sky consternates me; its
limpidity exasperates me. The insensitivity of the sea,
the immutability of the whole scene revolts me . . .
Ah! is it necessary to suffer eternally, or to flee the
beautiful eternally? Nature, pitiless enchantress, rival
always victorious, let me go! Refrain from tempting
my desires and my pride! The study of the beautiful is
a duel where the artist screams in terror before being
vanquished.

The *"Confiteor"* begins with delight in a season and a time: "How penetrating the ends of autumn days are!" and concludes, in the last paragraph, with consternation, exasperation, and terror in the face of the otherwise delicious penetration. With a view to the reversal in the last paragraph it is well to ask how these opening lines form the proper setting of the poem. There is a twofold pregnant synthesis: it is the *ends* of the days, and ends are also beginnings in temporal developments; more important perhaps, it is autumn, the end of summer and the beginning of winter. In each case something is to be born: the evening and the winter. The paradox of life and death, death and life, is a common theme of poetry and prose alike, but it is less common that evening and autumn, rather than dawn and spring, are taken to convey the point. In a sense, then, the reversal presented directly in the last paragraph announces itself in the first—by its mood. Indeed, the whole first paragraph is an elaboration of this mood of being on the verge of a new turning, but a turning that does not hold out the promise of relief—a turning rather that portends disaster. The mood is first of all one of acute penetration: "Ah! penetrating to the point of pain!" The very word suggests the atmosphere as one in which something forcefully pertinent will be acting upon, moving in upon man—upon the artist. The tense suspension of this mood is immediately enhanced by the invocation of "the vague." What is vague stands somewhat between transparent lucidity and clouded opacity. In the sense in which Baudelaire means the word, it does not merely stand there, but rather foreshadows and foretells something—if only ambivalently. Thus the poet says: " . . . the vagueness of [these certain delicious sensations] does not exclude their intensity." The intensity here is that of the sensations, of the feeling or mood which senses an imminent or impending "penetration," along with its felt force and as yet unknown significance. Accordingly, it is this intensely penetrating but nevertheless vague "somewhat" upon which the initial and somehow abiding mood of this prose poem is focused. It is a "somewhat" which somehow transcends, but nonetheless cuts into, the idyllic scene typified by the "ends of the days in autumn." The last line of the first paragraph sums it all up: ". . . there is no jab sharper than that of the Infinite."

While in the first paragraph we have a vaguely defined scene intensely threatened by something, presumably the Infinite, the second paragraph develops this scene in some detail insofar as it seems to be secure from this threat. It is no coincidence that while the first paragraph ended with the Infinite, the second starts off immediately: "A great delight it is to drown one's glance in the immensity of the sky and the sea!" Here we have the concrete setting or place of the poem—in the midst of the vast infinitude or immensity of inscrutable nature. "The sky and the sea"—these two aspects of primordial nature form the arena in which the initial encounter with reality occurs. In this first phase of man's encounter with gigantic reality all the senses come in and bask in the natural spectacle. "Solitude, silence, incomparable chastity of the blue sky! a small quivering sail at the horizon, which by its smallness and isolation imitates my irremediable existence, monotonous melody of the surf. . . ." Man becomes immersed in the sense impressions which nature showers on him. He feels cuddled into a resting order. He contemplates nature and melts into a reality perhaps deeper than the everyday. Everything seems to be dissolved into a unity of appearances. The boundaries between the self and the rest of the world, boundaries so prevalent in the frustrations of ordinary life, become dissipated: ". . . the *self* is soon lost!" However, as man feels at one with nature, something strange has happened to his senses: they have become means, or rather ends, in themselves; contrary to their function of being means *to* an end, as in ordinary experience, they no longer serve for anything beyond their own immediacy. In the sight of the "azur" and the sound of the surf, seeing and hearing are simply enjoyed. The sounds, smells, and sights do not indicate anything beyond this; they are what they are. Primordial nature becomes a temple of senses, a world of the senses in primordial unity. The usual distinction between a thinking subject and a thought about its object becomes meaningless: ". . . all these things think through me, or I think through them." This unity and lack of clear-cut distinction comes to a head in the last lines of the paragraph, where the immediacy of the sensuous presentation obliterates the traditional dichotomy between thought and things: ". . . they [the things] think, I say, but musically and picturesquely, without quibbles, without syllogisms, without deductions."

The third paragraph of the poem returns to the intensity of the mood, focusing on this as it evolves into a crisis: "But then these thoughts, whether they emerge from me, or spring from things, soon become too intense." The harmonious union of things thinking and things thought, the union between awe-inspiring nature and sensuous man, climaxes in its being *too* intense. As real, as delightful, as powerful as it may be, such harmonious unity between subject and object testifies to its own untenability. The very intensity and energy of these idyllic, pleasurable circumstances eventuates in its own contrary: "Energy within voluptuousness creates an uneasiness and a positive suffering." We shall notice that the poet speaks of the consequent suffering as positive. This qualification is contrary to our most ordinary ways of thinking. Why should the suffering be "positive"? This question may appear to be unanswerable from the context of the paragraph. However, we can see that *if* the suffering were in fact merely negative—contrary to what we read—it would function as an obliteration of man—much in the same way that the union of the previous paragraph eradicated the separate identity of man. For suffering is negative when it completely takes man over in such a way that only fruitless concentration on the pain and consequent self-pity result. Here, however, the qualification of suffering as positive suggests that it is going to function positively in the differentiation of man—or the artist, since he is the one who can in fact make something out of it—out of the idyllic mass of the initial encounter. As a result of the suffering, the narrator of the poem becomes aware that nature cannot be accepted on its own terms of immediacy—because those terms deny the identity of man—and furthermore that an activity or response of man is demanded if the encounter is to be grasped in its entire meaningfulness. For Baudelaire was much concerned to transform his "voluptuousness into knowledge" (B, 1215). The turning point of voluptuousness, on the one hand, and knowledge, on the other, is precisely where the perceiving subject distinguishes himself from his environment by the fact that his perceptions are peculiarly his and his alone, without finding their objects. Thus the last lines of the third paragraph leave the subject of the prose poem in this painful suspension and separation: "My too tensed nerves emit nothing but screaming and painful vibrations."

Finally, in the fourth and last paragraph, the harmonious union portrayed by the second paragraph is completely shattered. We have been warned by the poet, however, not to understand this disruption as negative, but rather to look for something positive. This would appear impossible at first sight: "And now the depth of the sky consternates me; its limpidity exasperates me." All sense impressions become the reverse of what they were before. The previously mysterious, immense, intense, incomparably chaste sky is now a source of consternation and exasperation. Furthermore, the pleasant melody of the sea has changed into "the insensitivity of the sea," and the penetration of the initial experience has evolved into a revolting "immutability of the whole scene." There is at this point, however, a break in the text, as though to suggest the introduction of something hitherto dormant. We read: "Ah! is it necessary to suffer eternally, or to flee the beautiful eternally?" Here we have, after the break indicated by the dots, the first direct reference to the fundamental element of art: the beautiful. But the text introduces this element not as an actuality already achieved but as a possibility apparently looming up for the first time, now, with the break with nature, with the break with reality as it has been hitherto encountered. The break may indeed appear negative on the face of it, but the passage just cited ("is it necessary to suffer eternally, or to flee the beautiful eternally?") indicates that this negation is pregnant with the vague possibility hinted at in the first paragraph and now clarified somewhat as the positive possibility of the beautiful, the condition of art itself. However, at this point in the development, the two possibilities stated are: *suffering* the beautiful or *fleeing* the beautiful; in either case no *relief* is offered—as is indeed suggested by the imagery in the first paragraph. What is poetically stated as a necessary condition of poetic development is a conflict in which man distinguishes himself from nature and is destined to succumb to the greater powers of the foe, in this case the nature or reality with which the narrator of the prose poem had previously enjoyed such a marvelous union and harmony: "Nature, pitiless enchantress, rival always victorious, let me go! Refrain from tempting my desires and my pride." Notice the peculiar character of the conflict: nature is a foe not because she is inherently evil and hateful (maintained by critics such as Sartre[7] and Auerbach[8]), but because there is somehow a temptation to become idyllically identified with her, and the consequent lack of self-identity is somehow untenable for the artist engaged in the creation of the work of art. And the beautiful, the defining characteristic of art, also makes no sense except within the conflict with this "most honorable enemy," a conflict in which the artist is precisely the one who is able to participate and cry out his work before his defeat. Thus we read in the last sentence: "The study of the beautiful is a duel where the artist screams in terror before being vanquished."

"*Le Confiteor de l'artiste*" is to be interpreted to convey what the title says. It is a prose poem embodying the "confession" of the artist, that is, the revelation of the creative process given by one who creates. In this we have an important example of the "self-consciousness" of poetry: a poem which is not only a poem but also a reflection upon itself, upon what it is, upon that which makes it what it is. We have up to now been considering the poem as a "reflection upon itself" and have seen it as reflecting an idyllic situation, haunted perhaps by a penetrating "somewhat," but characterized initially as a harmony and unity with nature, then as presently a crisis eventuating finally in a break containing both the emission of the artist's peculiar cry, his work, and his downfall. The poet indicates that the downfall is necessary, thereby implying that the emergence of the work of art, just as the harmonious union with nature, negates and obliterates the artist. But the point of this negation, what is "positive" in the suffering and eventual obliteration, is in no wise the enlightenment or salvation of the artist—more particularly the poet—but rather the work of art itself, the poem. Not the artist but rather the work of art survives. About this sole survivor nothing at all is said in the poem. But the "gap" in the confession should not surprise us. After all, the poem, this particular poem in front of us, "*Le Confiteor de l'artiste*," is precisely the point of the poem. It is this which fills the gap. Besides, each concretion of the creative process, as issuing from a breakaway from all that is predetermined and consequently independent of the passionate movement of the creative process, each new creation goes beyond any set rules or descriptions. Nevertheless, although a work of art does constitute a unity derived from a certain relationship vis-à-vis reality, and in the light of this derivation vividly presented by the "*Confiteor*," we can examine the status of the work of art as Baudelaire understood it, quite apart from any general prescription of its nature.

Paradoxically though, we must turn to Baudelaire's theoretical writings in order to gain an insight into the poetic concretions of the creative process. For each poem or work of art is its own concretion and cannot speak of another as its source. In any event, we can see how it might possibly be argued that Baudelaire's views on art have a theoretical foothold, if not a chronological beginning, in the experiences invoked and presented in the "*Confiteor*." For each paragraph of the prose poem seems to portray one moment of the emergence of art, to offer, enigmatically to be sure, the preconditions of art, and finally to make a suggestion as to its status. It is now necessary to underline, by referring to the poet's essays and letters, this suggested conception of art as it signals a break with reality, a destruction of it, and finally an autonomy and self-sufficiency of the work of art independent in some fundamental way of the reality from which it broke away.

The *"Confiteor"* ends with the downfall of the artist preceded by a positive suffering culminating in the lack of union and harmony previously enjoyed with nature. The break with the reality of nature is of course very clearly seen in Baudelaire's much celebrated distaste for the languid and idyllic nature of the Romanticists, and seen equally well in his opposition to Realism. It is, however, more interesting to note *why* the break is crucial for the artist and the work of art. Roughly speaking, the reason seems evident enough: the artist is not an artist if he merely *accepts* reality as it is; he must create something. Accordingly, Baudelaire says of the pure artist that he "sees mystery everywhere" (B, 706). And he asks: "What is a poet (I take this word in its widest meaning), if not a translator, a decipherer?" (B, 705). Furthermore, when speaking about different kinds of art, he refers to artists as "abstractors of quintessences": that is to say, the artist must abstract not only the essence from the reality of nature which he faces but also the "quintessence," that fifth essence of the Greeks which, though it contains all the physical elements of the world, is not itself physically or naturally present, but reveals itself only indirectly through the other four essences (B, 885). What is common to all these passages is the marked unwillingness to conceive of the artist or poet as one who absorbs nature; what interests the artist and poet is only revealed to him as he stands apart from nature and reality and carefully ferrets out his material from it. Because he both stands apart and also borrows from nature, however, the artist cannot simply divorce himself from her. Indeed, the last paragraph of the *"Confiteor"* speaks of nature as a "rival—always victorious." And in his theoretical writings we run across a strange passage which speaks, in passing, of beautiful painting as being "nature reflected by an artist" (B, 877). The double meaning of the verb "to reflect" suggests the problem at hand. First, to reflect means to think over—and this is precisely what the artist does when he takes a stand at a distance from reality before incorporating it into his creation. But the verb also means to reflect in the sense in which a mirror reflects the image of that which happens to be placed in front of it. This sense of the word suggests that the reality of nature *somehow* abides in art, if only as a reminder to the effect that she is not going to be, and was not originally, accepted at her face value. However, this sense of "reflecting nature" is destined to remain weak, even though we are probably inclined to accept it as the stronger of the two. For Baudelaire is on the whole quite clear about his belief that the artist must recoil from the temptations of languishing in nature. Although it is made quite clear in the *"Confiteor,"* the *Salon de 1846,* in the section on eclecticism and doubt, states it concisely: " . . . the first task of an artist is to substitute man for nature and to protest against her" (B, 930).

That the artist must break off from temptations to become absorbed in the initial shower of impressions falling down upon him from nature, that he has to stand aside and channel the ever-changing flux of sensations into a definite and definitive direction, that he has to pick his materials out of nature rather than accept her at face value—all are evident in, "Nature . . . is nothing but an incoherent mass of materials which the artist is called upon to associate and to put in order, it is an *incitamentum,* an awakening of the slumbering faculties!" (B, 1124) In other words, natural reality being chaotic and incoherent, the emergence of art presupposes a distance from which the artist can wrestle from this mass a special possibility of creation. Similarly we read Baudelaire's comment: "The entire universe is merely a storehouse of images and signs to which the imagination assigns a relative place and value" (B, 1044). Art is man's attempt to assert himself by forming the natural materials of his experience, by giving the manifold appearances a new order— or giving them an order for the first time—and by creating a unity from plurality. This may all seem evident enough, but these passages actually contain the paradoxical implication that the artist breaks with the reality of nature only to return to it, and returns to it only to break from it. One is reminded here of what Camus says with respect to the artist's ambivalent position vis-à-vis reality: "The world is nothing and the world is everything, such is the double and unwearying scream of every true artist."[9] And that, consequently, the artist's experience of the world is "a perpetually renewed dissension."[10]

Granting for the present that some sort of break with nature and reality characterizes the process by which the work of art comes into being, what guarantees that this break actually resides in the completed and produced work of art? Could the break not confine itself to the mere method by which the artist gathers his materials, a method destined to be left behind by the result? Perhaps this question cannot be fully answered until the self-sufficiency of the work has been developed and clarified. However, one part of the *"Confiteor"* can serve to suggest the hypothesis that the break does in fact abide: "Ah! is it necessary to suffer eternally, or to flee the beautiful eternally?" It makes no difference where beauty may be found, in nature or in art, the same dilemma is also found, the dilemma of either fleeing or suffering. In either case, a break seems to be concomitant to beauty. If this hypothesis is confirmed, namely, that the finished work of art retains this character of a break with reality (when considered as art and not as merchandise for the art dealer or as amusement for the distraction of the bored public), then the work of art would in some sense include a destruction of the reality from which it broke away—at least to the extent that it also claims a status of its own. And Baudelaire does seem to hold that a destruction is implied by the creation of art: in the third chapter of *Salon de 1859,* "The Queen of Faculties," he describes the inadequacy of the copy theory of art in light of this queen of the faculties, the imagination. In sum the argument states that no factual, learned, or passively received set of data from nature suffices in itself for the emergence of authentic art. The queen of faculties must be called into play: "The imagination touches upon all the others [faculties]; it excites them, it sends them into battle" (B, 1037-38). He then goes on to describe the way in which it functions: "It decomposes all of creation, and with the materials gathered and arranged according to rules which originate only in the farthest depths of the soul, it creates a new world, it produces the sensation of the new. Since it created the world . . . , it is only just that it govern it."[11]

For our purposes, it will be instructive to concentrate on the three statements: "it decomposes all of creation," "it creates a new world," and, finally, "it is only just that it govern it." *All* of nature is decomposed, deformed, or destroyed for the sake of a *new* world to be created, and the same principle of decomposition and creation should prevail in the finished product, just as it *does* as a matter of fact prevail in the process by which it is produced. It is clearly implied, if not explicitly stated, that the work of art not only disregards the original, that is, the ordinary order of things but also rules over all things (in so far as it is seen as a work of art) and actually invalidates, that is, destroys in some sense that other order. It is interesting that Baudelaire does not keep up the symmetry of his previous statements, and that, instead of saying imagination *does* govern the world it created, he says rather that it is *just* that it governs it, implying that there is an injustice in those instances where this rule does not prevail.

It is not obvious how Baudelaire actually incorporated his views on decomposition and sovereignty into his poetry. Perhaps he wanted to say only that the real work of art, whether it happens to be classical or modern, already displays these qualities by the very fact that it is art, and that these qualities may be either covert or overt. In any event, we can see a certain subtle violation of our ordinary views of life and beauty by the title of Baudelaire's best known work, *Les Fleurs du mal*. The poet wrote in one of the projected prefaces that the task of this work was ". . . to extract *beauty* from *Evil*" (B, 185). Here we have a proposal the mere possibility of which goes contrary to our normal preconceptions and expectations, not to mention those ordinarily entertained at the time of Baudelaire. If the title had implied that the poems of the volume were the flowers or fruits of goodness, there would have been no tacit claim either to have destroyed the ordinary reality in which we are generally engrossed or to govern the realm out of which the poems were extracted. However, as it is, the title claims that the poems were derived from a source which is itself ordinarily discredited as a bona fide realm of beauty. We might then conclude that if these flowers do in fact reign, as the poet would have it, they owe no allegiance to the ordinary realm, but by contrast rule over that realm.

That the emergence of the work of art entails a break with ordinary reality comes out still more clearly as we consider a third point prevalent in his theoretical writings. The break of art from natural reality implies and involves not only a *destruction* or decomposition of that reality away from which the work of art breaks but also a *self-sufficiency* of the reality which the work itself constructs. Briefly, Baudelaire sees art as an end in itself, a kind of absolute. Poetry is sufficient unto itself. "Poetry must not, under penalty of death or degradation, assimilate itself to science or to morality; it does not have Truth as its end, it has only Itself" (B, 685). In other words, he says, "Poetry has nothing but itself as its end." Here we have one of the first concise and decisive formulations of the autonomy of the work of art, more specifically the work of poetry. Art and poetry were traditionally regarded as functioning variously in the communication of social norms or ideals, as embodying the essences of the human, the natural, or the divine, or as expressing the dramatic view of life as it is experienced by the soul of a sensitive poet. Nobody would deny that such functions can and have been discerned, but Baudelaire maintains that the essence and real function of art and poetry are missed by any view which focuses its attention upon one or more of them. This is the theoretical point which is made over and over again in the modern trend of art and poetry since Baudelaire, sometimes to the point of deliberate absurdity as in the case of much contemporary art. But even though we may see a correlation between Baudelaire's theory and modern practice, it still remains to be seen whether Baudelaire actually embodied his principles in his own poetry. To consider this question, we shall examine once again the *"Confiteor."*

The last "verse" or sentence of the *"Confiteor"* suggests something about both the status of art and the situation of the artist: "The study of the beautiful is a duel where the artist screams in terror before being vanquished." Why does the poem speak of the *study* of the beautiful when we might expect to hear something about the *creation* of the beautiful? The implications of the respective alternatives are divergent. To study the beautiful implies that the object of study, whether it be nature or art, somehow exists independently of the man or the men concerned with it. In this case the autonomy of beauty and art is preserved. But the other alternative, to create the beautiful, raises with some ambiguity the question whether or not the work of art is entirely dependent upon the creator, and whether or not it can be properly explained by referring to the personality of the artist. We speak loosely of the artist as originating or creating his work, but Baudelaire seems to suggest that this is misleading. This suggestion is bolstered by the ending of the sentence: the artist is vanquished. On the face of it, this seems to tell us something of the plight of the artist and to reduce the work of art to the situation of the artist, thereby disclaiming art as an absolute. But this interpretation would only hold up if art *contained* the plight of the artist. As a matter of fact, the poem claims that the beautiful, or the work of art, *results* in the plight of the artist.

Far from containing the personality of the would-be creator, art rejects him and says nothing more about him than that he is so rejected. With this rejection in mind, it would seem strange to maintain that Baudelaire's conception of art was such that the work would be destined to give form to his own peculiar "state of mind." His critics have, however, done an exhaustive job of showing Baudelaire's similarities with the Romantic poets on this point, basing their arguments on the fact that the artist is still considered in this oblique way to figure in the work, and that Baudelaire himself said he still suffered from the stigma of Romanticism. Nonetheless, we must speak here about that which distinguishes Baudelaire and enables him to re-form the Romantic heritage into a thought and poetry which is powerful enough to engender subsequent trends in these subjects.

If Baudelaire wanted *Les Fleurs du mal* to be seen as a poetry of personal confessions or a diary of his private states of being, he did not make his desire explicit; he did not date his poems in the fashion Victor Hugo did, nor are there any overt references to personages and events in his own life. In fact, he writes in a letter to Calonne (November 1858) that he purposely avoided introducing such references. After speaking of some attempts that had been made to interpret his poetry in a religious vein, thereby detracting from their autonomy, he states: "Only those endowed with an absolute bad faith will fail to understand the intentional impersonality of my poetry."[12] Even though most of the poems of *Les Fleurs du mal* do in fact speak in the "I" form, the form by itself does not justify any judgment personalizing the poetry. This form is a technique of narration, and it is the entire narration as such that constitutes the work of poetry in its autonomy. Baudelaire conceives of this narration as a function of what he calls the imagination, and not as a function of either the heart or the rational powers of man. That is, poetry cannot be reduced to either subjective or objective elements outside the work itself: "Thus the principle of poetry is strictly and simply the human aspiration toward a superior Beauty, and the manifestation of this principle lies in an enthusiasm . . . [which] is completely independent of passion, or the intoxication of the heart, and independent of truth, or the fodder of reason" (B, 686). In the same essay he continues: "The sensitivity of the heart can even be harmful in this case. The sensitivity of the imagination is of a different nature; it knows how to choose, how to judge, how

to compare, how to flee this, how to search out that, rapidly, spon-
taneously" (B, 688). The point of these passages is that the narration of a poem may be characterized by enthusiasm and imagination, but in a way which allows it to stand in its own right, apart
from distractions from the side either of the poet or of any supposed
reality external to the narration. In accordance with this enigmatic
transcendence, Baudelaire concludes by ascribing a paradoxical
motto to the poet: "My function is extra-human" (B, 700).

Both as a poet *and* as an aesthetician, Baudelaire made con-
siderable contribution to the course and understanding of art, but
we must nevertheless admit that in his work the tendencies and
trends of modern art and aesthetics are still embryonic in form.
More than that, of course, it is evident that much of what he has to
say remains couched in traditional terms. But as Rimbaud remarked
of any poet, "other horrible workers will come; they will begin at the
horizons where he succumbed!" (R, 271) Examples of these "horrible workers" are easy enough to recall; we have only to think of
Valéry and his belief that poetry, breaking away from the usual view
of existence, was "a perfectly constructed fragment of an inexistent
edifice."[13] And then we can recall that Surrealism rightly deduced
its name and the aim of its movement from Baudelaire's "surna-
turalism."

Other poets immediately succeeding Baudelaire deliberately
implement the element of destruction into their work in blatant
ways. Mallarmé's obscure poetry, for instance, frustrates any attempt
to correlate systematically his verses with ordinary aspects of experience. Mallarmé's view of the language of poetry carries Baudelaire's
hesitant remarks to their logical conclusion: the poetic phrase no
longer names the presence of things, but destroys them while relying on a presentation of their absence.[14]

Rimbaud, who speaks of Baudelaire as "the first visionary,
King of poets, *a real God,*" brings these ideas into further concretion
(R, 273). *Les Illuminations* offers testimony that poetry can free
itself from any and all external shackles, and can stand in front of
us as a pure absolute paying no homage to any other power but
itself. The depersonalization which had started with Baudelaire
emerges here in its purest form. For most of the poems in *Les
Illuminations* have no "I" at all and hardly any reference to reality
as we ordinarily conceive of it with our ordinary concepts of order

and meaning. In those poems where we do find "I," it would be hard to maintain that the author was meant.[15]

Baudelaire's approach to poetry and art, the approach involving a break with and a destruction of ordinary reality, leads in the direction of a conception of all art as an absolute and gives it an independent status. Here we find one of the first movements to create an art concentrating on its own essence and drawn toward itself. This is the birth of the remarkable phenomenon of modern art, where neither the artist nor the "states of mind" of the artist nor the values upon which our world is erected stand in the foreground. It is an art dedicated to an absolute, to which neither natural forms nor the interests of man nor formal aesthetic worries can give a name. This absolute is art itself.

mallarmé's poetic transformation

In 1868 Mallarmé writes to François Copée: "And now, having arrived at the horrible vision of the pure work, I have about lost my mind and all contact with the meaning of the most common ways of speaking."[19] The poet is personally testifying that he strives toward an ideal work of language and, in doing so, tends to move away from ordinary forms of everyday speech. He also implies that this direction of movement is fraught with difficulties for him: it is somehow horrible to behold the goal. This duality of the ideal and the ordinary lies in the very nature of language according to Mallarmé, who writes: "An undeniable urge of my time is to separate, in view of divergent attributes, the twofold status of language: on the one hand, the crude or immediate, and, on the other hand, the essential" (M, 368). This simple bifurcation is the beginning of a theory of language. It raises, however, a number of important questions. What is language in its "raw" aspects? What is language in its "essential" aspects? And what is the relationship between the two that makes the vision "horrible"?

Mallarmé answers these questions at the end of his commentary "Crise de vers" (M, 368):

> Narration, teaching, even description is all right, although for each of these it would perhaps suffice, in order to exchange human thought silently to take from or put into another person's hand a money coin: the elementary usage of discourse serves universal *reportage* in which every contemporary genre of writing partakes, with the exception of literature.

Language appears usually as a medium of exchange similar to money. It serves to transfer human thought from one person to another and back again. The predominant feature of such discourse is that all value is placed on the things about which men speak. Like money, language is itself worthless; it receives its worth according to its referents, and these in turn receive their worth according to human interests such as are summed up in man's commercial life. Language thus serves a purpose at this level, and a necessary one at that. It is basically a reporting, and under this heading comes not only the obvious, such as gossiping, but also common kinds of uses, such as "narrating, instructing, and even describing." In other words, Mallarmé's view of ordinary, crude, or immediate language covers every sort except the truly literary or poetic. Indeed, one wonders what is left for essential language if even narrating and describing are forbidden.

Rather than functioning definitely in the world of ordinary human concerns, language is said to receive its ultimate meaning and justification in terms of its ability, in the hands of the poet, to form and devise its own world. Thus Mallarmé goes on to say:

> Contrary to functioning as an easy and representative mode of currency, as the crowd would have it, speaking—being above all dream and song—recovers its virtuality with the poet, who is necessarily defined by an art devoted to fictions.

Here we have a statement of the radical creativity involved in language: if it seems to report something, as it does ordinarily, it must be seen more basically, i.e, "essentially," as producing rather than copying its subject matter. Essential language is then poetry by definition.

Mallarmé asserts that any and all language enjoys its virtuality, its power and validity, owing to its poetic or "essential" character. The appearance of language in its everyday commercial (crude and immediate) aspect is its degeneration. This order of ranking states, in effect, that the poet cannot begin with ordinary patterns of human speech and work them into poetry. Poetry is not everyday language warmed over and embellished. Everyday language is language that has lost contact with its primal origin. Its merely apparent and ultimately false origin is henceforth the domain of human interests and motivations. It would follow that the world of fiction created by the poet must be one which abstracts from the man who tells of it, one which lets the words speak for themselves.[20] Mallarmé therefore says: "The pure work implies the voiced disappearance of the poet who cedes the initiative to the words . . ." (M, 268). The poet disappears and the words take over. We ordinarily speak with the opposing purpose of letting the words disappear for the sake of satisfying our human interests. In July 1868, Mallarmé writes to Henri Cazalis a comment on one of his own sonnets: "I extract this sonnet . . . from a projected study on *Speech:* it is inverse,—I mean that the meaning . . . is evoked by an inner mirage of the words themselves. By murmuring it several times to oneself one experiences a rather cabalistic sensation."[21] Ordinary speaking is thus the exact inverse of true speaking. The poet, although he is a man, must draw upon and serve the world of words and sacrifice the ordinary human world. It is no wonder that Mallarmé experiences horror at the threshold of the "pure work" so understood.[22]

The theory that true (or poetic) language creates and so *is* its own world must still account for a subject matter. In Hegelian fashion, Mallarmé holds that poetic language gives itself its own content.[23] Poetic speech is kinetic rather than static: it is movement which continuously runs up against what confronts man as other than man. But since what confronts man is what it is only in the movement, the language can be said to determine its own subject matter. Self-conscious of its responsibility to provide its own content, poetic language constantly recalls the possibility of its own failure: the possibility of there being no content at all, the possibility of nothingness.

In a letter to Cazalis, July 1866, Mallarmé remarks: "I am in truth on a voyage, but in unknown lands, and if like to evoke cold images in order to escape from torrid reality I should tell you that for a month now I have been in the purest glaciers of Aesthetics—that after having found nothingness, I have found the beautiful—and that you cannot imagine the lucid altitudes in which I venture."[24] He goes on to say that a poem resulted from this voyage; and that the subject matter of poetry derives from nothingness, comes out in cold images, and stands in contrast to torrid reality. The poet does not embellish this ordinary reality; he sees in this only a nothingness occasioning a poetic movement of language with its own reality. Instead of founding the work of language in any way upon elements of already existing reality, this theory says that the poetic work arises from the realization and experience of this reality as nothing in itself.

In 1867 in a letter to the poet Villiers de L'Isle Adam, Mallarmé describes his experience of nothingness when thinking about his future work. He explains how he would like to write two books, one on "Beauty" and the other on "Sumptuous Allegories about Nothingness." But he bewails the fact that he has lost the "power of evoking, in a unique nothingness, an emptiness disseminated in its porousness." Thus, failing to do justice to the "ineffaceable notion of pure Nothingness," he writes: "The mirror reflecting Being toward me has most often been Horror." He goes on to explain that his personal experience of his impotence in the face of nothingness was one of exhaustion and pain.[25]

Mallarmé does not seem interested, however, in dwelling upon the negative and fruitless experience of nothingness. He feels that poetic creativity consists of the ability of language to work the experience of nothingness into something positive, into an experience of the pure "notion": "What good is the marvel of transposing a fact of nature into its virtual vibratory disappearance according to the play of words—if it isn't so that the pure notion will emanate from it without the impediment of an approximate or concrete recollection" (M, 368). There are two phases of the play of words here: the near negation of things, and the act of allowing their purity to emerge into clarity. We ordinarily think of the poetic word as pointing to things, as making them explicit, as drawing them out of their everyday penumbra into the light. Mallarmé claims the exact opposite: things in their ordinary penumbra must, by the poetic word, be even more overshadowed in order that something more real might emanate from the obscurity. In other words, the poetic word does not point to things: insofar as it points, it points to nothingness. Rather than making things be, the poet *lets* and *leaves* them be. It follows that such poetry would be inaccessible to a literary approach which desired to explicate what objects of experience the poems were meant to indicate, describe, or elicit. This accounts, at least in part, for the difficulty encountered in reading Mallarmé's poetry.[26]

We run headlong into the crux of this theory when we ask what exactly is the pure notion or, rather, how exactly does it loom into view. Mallarmé exemplifies what he means by essential or poetic language when he writes: "I say: a flower! and the one that is absent from all bouquets, the gentle idea itself, comes forth musically—beyond the oblivion where my voice relegates no contour—inasmuch as it is something different from all known calyxes" (M, 368). The essential feature of poetic speech lies in its ability to evoke "the gentle idea itself," the pure notion, as something not even invoked from the memory of previously known things, as something presupposing the oblivion or nothingness of these things. But does this mean that poetry is to thrive on barren abstractions, dull and divorced from concrete existence? In other words, does the poetic world of language preclude the possibility of our playing a concrete and appreciative role in it? At first sight it might seem to. Mallarmé is evidently insisting, however, that we have a stake in this gentle idea, this pure notion; for he says that it comes forth or arises "musically." This term implies a fullness of human experience even if, perhaps even insofar as it is not defined by any "known calyxes," that is, by previous experiences, interests, and motivations. It follows that the so-called abstraction is neither barren nor dull. By the same token it would seem evident that it is something very close to concrete existence. To be sure, what is concrete cannot be identified here with what is ordinary or "pecuniary" in the imagery cited before. The concrete is rather a character of existence which is set to man as a task, something to be searched out and worked for. Thus in a letter dated June 1884, we read: "Poetry is the expression of the mysterious sense of the aspects of existence by means of human language brought back to its essential rhythm; in this way it endows our everyday life with an authenticity and constitutes the only spiritual task."[27] Essential language expresses neither aspects of existence nor existence itself, but the mysterious sense of these.

Since Mallarmé is working within Hegelian terminology in struggling to state his views, it is helpful to remember how Hegel himself understood the terms *idea* and *notion*. According to him, all human activity is basically thinking, and any moment of thinking is a thought: that is, a rule of thumb, a generality, a universal that is divorced from and awaiting its particular content. In contrast to thought (*Gedanke* as a product of *Denken*), a notion (*Begriff*) is this same thought as it grapples with and is in the process (movement) of grasping (*greifen*) the given, namely, what a man is actually confronting. A notion is thus basically kinetic and concrete; it is the kinetic concretion of an otherwise abstract thought. In fact, any concrete experience, whether in sport or labor, is notional (conceptual) in Hegel's sense. Thoughts all by themselves are essentially idle. Philosophical contemplation is not interested in the products and aftereffects of thinking, nor is it exemplified in mere thoughts. To contemplate is rather to undertake the movement of notional experience *explicitly* and for its own sake. In this way the notions come out in their purity: pure concrete notions become visions, what have been called ideas in philosophy since Plato. An idea is then not something a man looks at (Plato), nor something a man harbors in himself (Descartes), nor a generality extracted and left over from experience (Hume): it is a self-determining and concrete movement of the spirit. Finally, the motivation for the movement itself, as well as the individual's development from mere thoughts to concrete notions to contemplative ideas, is the actual experience of nothingness: the dialectical experience that every time an abstraction (thought) or a grasping (notion) is completed, the content vanishes and man is left with an emptiness which can only be filled if he gives himself up to concrete, self-determining activity once again. Hegel understood this activity largely in terms of labor and language.[28]

Language in its essence creates its own world and is its own standard. Mallarmé even suggests that it creates the real world in its mystery. Since language is the medium and essence of poetry, its creation poses a peculiar problem: how can it be understood, since it can not be definitely related to anything outside of itself? The poet quite literally has nothing to rely upon, but this "nothing" has two meanings here. First, it means that the poet's language is neither based upon nor derived from things. It relates to what is absent from things as they already exist, namely, to their idea in its purity. Second, it means that poetry issues from and so reminds us of the meaninglessness, the nothingness of the world apart from linguistic creativity; poetry emerges in the face of horror.[29] This double aspect of the problem of poetry is summed up in a brief note jotted down by Mallarmé in 1869: "In poetic language—just show that the purpose of language is to become beautiful and not to express the Beautiful among other things . . ." (M, 353). The experience of beauty stands opposed to the experience of nothingness and meaninglessness; it is what makes life worthwhile. And yet this beauty is not first found and then expressed; it comes into being first and foremost in language itself. For Mallarmé, in and through verse both language and things come into their true being.

Mallarmé's formulation for the transformation of poetry reads: " . . . to transpose a fact of nature into its near disappearance, virtual and vibratory, according to the play of speech" (M, 368). What happens in this transformation? The poet answers this question in some detail as follows:

> Verse, remaking from several words a total new word which is alien to language and like an incantation, achieves a peculiar isolation of the word: it denies, with a sovereign stroke, the element of chance which remained in these terms even after they have been alternately dipped into meaning and sonority, and it gives you the surprise of having never before heard such an ordinary fragment of voiced language, while at the same time *the reminiscence of the named object bathes in a new atmosphere.* (italics ours)

What happens, in short, is a "new atmosphere." For Mallarmé this atmosphere is not achieved primarily by a convincing articulation of a fictitious image. Although it may require such an articulation as well, the power lies in another dimension. Instead of stating the way things are, the poetic articulation hails their withdrawal. Partaking of this articulation, we as poetic readers find ourselves drawn out of our familiar view of things. Most poets would probably agree that poetic speech somehow overcomes, transcends, dissolves, or modifies our familiar view of things. Mallarmé's peculiar claim is that the power of the familiar is broken not by something unfamiliar being presented, or something being presented in an unfamiliar way: rather it is broken as given and familiar things are absented. Not presentation, but "absentation": "near disappearance, virtual and vibratory." The verge of withdrawal is articulated with a power and vibration which draws us along, too. We are present by virtue of our reminiscence. However, this reminiscence, instead of serving to harbor thoughts within ourselves, is drawn out into the fresh air of a new world.

In the passage quoted above, Mallarmé says that poetic transformation happens in and through verse which remakes, denies, and surprises. It is only in verse that we can actually see and hear what the poet means. Let us look at the soonet *"A la nue accablante,"* the penultimate poem in the volume Mallarmé was preparing for publication when he died in 1898. It had appeared in 1895 in the Berlin journal *Pan* (cf. M, 76, 1501).

A LA NUE ACCABLANTE

A la nue accablante tu
Basse de basalte et de laves
A même les échos esclaves
Par une trompe sans vertu

Quel sépulcral naufrage (tu
Le sais, écume, mais y baves)
Suprême une entre les épaves
Abolit le mât dévêtu

Ou cela que furibond faute
De quelque perdition haute
Tout l'abîme vain éployé

Dans le si blanc cheveu qui traîne
Avarement aura noyé
Le flanc enfant d'une sirène.

A LA NUE ACCABLANTE

Untold to the oppressing cloud
Low with basalt and lavas
Neither to the slavish echoes
Through a powerless tuba

What a sepulchral shipwreck (you
Know it, O foam, but you spit thereon)
One supreme among the derelicts
Destroys the naked mast

Or only this; furious, lacking
Some high perdition
The entire vain abyss gaping

In the hair so white which floats
Greedily will have drowned
The childlike body of a siren.

The poem makes for difficult reading and comprehension. Yet the theme is a fairly familiar one. The poem tells of the sea, or rather the events of the sea. Images from the sea are often favorites in literature; we think of Homer in ancient times, and of Joyce, Conrad, Hemingway, and others in more recent times. Mallarmé's own poem "Salut" (M, 27), placed as an exergue prefacing the volume of his poetry which first appeared posthumously, addresses his fellow poets in the image of a ship at sea—mentioning neither ship nor sea, but instead component images such as foam and sirens. And his masterful *"Un Coup de Dés"* (M, 455-77), with detailed imagery corresponding in some respects (notably the shipwreck) to our poem, is situated directly over the gaping abyss of the sea. However, ours is not a seafaring poem; it does not tell of a human adventure. We are confronted with a seascape rather than a cruise and search. The overall impression avoids conveying human striving or moral concern. Instead it is an impression of puzzling absence. This strange absence, moreover, does not draw attention to the personality of the narrator of the poem. Simply by suggesting a familiar theme and then proceeding to direct it contrary to ordinary expectations, Mallarmé undoes the forces of the familiar.

Apart from some contortion in the syntax, the individual images are fairly comprehensible: something has happened, although what can now be seen (the cloud) and heard (the tuba=the roar of the sea?) remains unexplained (first stanza). Next we perceive a shipwreck, known but scorned by the foam, and a barren mast being destroyed by the greatest of the derelicts (second stanza). Alternatively, it is suggested that perhaps only the fury of the sea exists, vainly distending its abyss, lacking any real effect (third stanza). Finally, the fourth stanza recalls the mythical image of a siren who will yet be drowned in the "hair so white" (the foam?).

"A verse," Mallarmé says, "denies, with a sovereign stroke, the element of chance" in the words. The verses of *"A la nue accablante"* bring words into contact with one another in such a way that their meanings intersect to purge each other of their familiar purport. In the first stanza the cloud is weighted down with black volcanic rock and the echoes are enslaved: from a commonsense point of view, one image is physically impossible and the other is a fantastic anthropomorphism. Similarly, in the second stanze human possibilities (knowing, scornful spitting) are attributed to natural phenomena (the foaming of the sea). The last two stanzas purge the poem of any remaining security of image. The first tercet suggests that perhaps there is no shipwreck at all, but only the fury of the sea. The second tercet projects the death of a drowned siren, a purely mythical figure in the context of what might have otherwise been fact even if unclear. And then, too, each stanza articulates a distinctly different mood: first, a sense of oppressive ignorance; second, a sense of disaster coupled with defiance; third, anger and engulfment; fourth, dreamy sadness. We are thus given several differing ways of reacting to the scene. The intentional ambiguity of the overall visual image and felt sentiment shows that "denying chance" means something directly contrary to achieving a clear meaning. Evidently, the words in the verses liberate one another from the indifference characterizing their meaning insofar as they serve ordinary and chance purposes in our everyday experience. They thus stand ready to serve a higher purpose.

"Verse," Mallarmé also says, remakes "from several words a total new word which is . . . like an incantation." Although the poetic reader of the poem is deliberately rendered insecure about both the images and the moods, he is nonetheless firmly secured within its ambiguous meaning by its recurrent sonority. The poem as a whole is a single word which initially captures and occupies our attention like cantos in obscure languages do: we are enrapt without any clear idea of what the meaning is. *"A la nue accablante"* evokes a multitude of images with a variety of moods, however, and our glance is effectively drawn upon the experience of the seascape (unless, of course, for some personal reason, we become indignant at the language). The poem prevents us from responding in the usual way, i.e., from recognizing chance elements and thereby reducing the meanings of the words to familiar categories. But the poem gives us a medium and a direction of response:

the medium being the available images and moods and the direction being the sea itself, deliberately left unnamed.

"Verse gives you the surprise of having never before heard such an ordinary fragment of voiced language," Mallarmé finally says. The surprise is that in this poem the sea emerges for what it is in quite ordinary language: there are no neologisms in this case, and the poem is hardly a calligram. *"A la nue accablante"* is extraordinary not because its words have complex meanings but because these words converge upon an immediate content just as it is. The sea presents itself in this way: withdrawing from each and every possible meaning, every preferred image and mood. The sea is indeed a "fact of nature." However, we seldom experience it as such. Rather, we approach it according to how we are supposed to experience it: an occasion for adventure in popular tales, for excitement and pleasure of surfing and seduction in adolescence, for rhythmical relaxation in old age. A stormy sea recalls and suggests all these meanings, including those of disaster, myth, and silence, but it specifies none. The sea is always something more than the meanings it bears. For Mallarmé, this something more is experienced as it withdraws, with power and vibration, from these meanings. The thing itself presents itself in the mode of "absentation": near disappearance.

The transformation peculiar to poetry, as understood by Mallarmé as both thinker and poet, drives us into a reconsideration of the human involvement in language. Ordinarily, if not traditionally, language is taken simply as embodying the significance of things. We like to think that in our linguistic involvements we arrange meanings to arrive at a cogent picture of the way things are. The problematics of higher or better language then arises in meeting the need to pave the way toward higher and better meanings, or at least (in these days of nihilism) a more accurate arrangement of them. Thus we might assume that *"A la nue accablante"* should present either an embellishment of familiar meanings in a seascape, or perhaps a veiled statement of a deeper significance of things for man. But significances in themselves, no matter how deep, will veil their signification. For example, excessive knowledge *about* the cathedral of Chartres may prevent us from actually seeing it directly. Significance, on the other hand, is the recognition of familiar connections serving, positively or negatively, the human pursuit and the fulfillment of human needs. And yet signification is the sole genuine support of significances and, when lost to them, leaves us in despairing oblivion. The real task of language then, is not to pursue new meanings or better arrangements of old meanings. It is to articulate its meanings, open them out on what withdraws from them and yet provides them with the momentary support proper to them.

Poetry is essentially problematic. Theories of language identical with or akin to that of Mallarmé haunt almost every quarter of linguistic creativity today. We have lost all naive confidence in the old belief that man is naturally endowed with the capacity to speak truly, effectively, and sometimes even poetically. Roland Barthes sums up this contemporary trend concisely when he says: "For a long time, the classical-bourgeois society has seen in the word an instrument or a decoration; now we see in it a sign and a truth. Everything that is touched upon by language is thus called into question: philosophy, the humanities, literature."[30] Ernest Gellner similarly points out the crisis in the cultural domain of language: "The use of language and of ordinary concepts has lost its confidence and its innocence. ...The heightened sense of language, the self-consciousness in the employment of it, the urgent desire to find theories as legitimizing or correcting it, the sense of an abyss of meaninglessness ever yawning, and viciously camouflaged, under our feet—all this springs from the fact that the humanist culture itself, the life of the word, the confidence in its capacity to relate to reality, is threatened."[31]

There is nothing natural about essential language any more. Rather than resulting from a reflection of meanings already available, poetry remains and comes into being as a challenge and a problem, a reflection of language within itself, a speaking and writing which evokes the absence of things in the mode of a supportive "absentation."

mallarmé and the experience of art

Mallarmé called the one book he himself published *Divagations;* it appeared in 1897 and comprised all of the prose poems he had then finished and most of the strictly prose works that had been published in various journals up to that time. In the note prefacing this collection we are told that the work brings to the fore "a unique subject, that of thought" (M, 1538). The book itself he does not like, we are told in the same note. Such a thing has no architecture, and whatever it offers is fragmented. It is like a monastery in ruins: it exhales something of its "doctrine" to the man who has chosen to pick and find his way, in around, and through the remains, relying perhaps more on his nostrils than on his eyes. The subject of these fragments is art. The choice of subject is not surprising, since Mallarmé was himself a poet. But even as a poet he could hardly refrain from thinking about the problems of interpreting art; he is a thinker as well as an artist; he thinks the experience of art as well as creates it. But at the same time he knows that his job is not to substitute an intellectual exegesis for the experience itself. The "doctrine" must remain something of a mystery. It can preserve its subject only by effacing itself. More than that, the "doctrine" must suggest the experience as it defies reduction to an intellectual exegesis; it must itself suggest the mystery. The image is well chosen—a monastery in ruins: something divine in origin and intention and yet secular in fact. The truest reconstruction is the most momentary and fleeting.

The title *Divagations* is playful. It comes from a verb meaning to digress, to meander about. It suggests a slow and yet carefree pace, and so a special way of attempting to understand its subject, namely art. The kind of thinking requisite for understanding art must be one that floats to and fro with the fluctuations of the experience of art. For the experience here is that of life itself, life as emergent, alive, and becoming, and the thinking which remains true to it must flow with it, enter into its play, and beware of the prudish attitude of aloofness which inevitably attends reflective thought as its supreme temptation. Such thinking can build no castles, and therefore has no real architecture of its own. If it is to remain true to the building and architecture of which it speaks, its own structure must remain transparent to what it is talking about. A treatise on aesthetics tends to become opaque to the experience of art; it sets out to prove an interest in itself. The title *Divagations* describes a different task: that of directing attention and interest onto what it is that gives rise to the thought, onto the experience of art. The work stands already as an antithesis, or perhaps more positively as an antidote, to the then current development of aesthetic theory. In an essay on Whistler's *Ten O'Clock,* Mallarmé speaks apocalyptically: "The voice of the aesthetician can now be heard over the land, and catastrophe impends" (M, 579). Before him, Hegel had argued that "in regard to its highest destiny and truest meaning, art remains for us something of the past."[32] Once theories evolve which try to justify the appearance of art on the human scene, or which try to explain its meaning to us, the experience of art has indeed died out; only some kind of resuscitation is possible, if that.

What strikes the reader of Mallarmé's writings as most immediately intelligible is the fact that he tries unremittingly to do something that has not been done. From then on, however, the reader tends to find him unintelligible, particularly if one takes as unintelligible that which is contrary to the familiar and ordinary. His concern is more than simply avant-garde. Baudelaire was certainly ahead of his own time, particularly in his reflective and critical writings, but he can be read easily enough since he continues to employ familiar categories, doing so in new ways. Mallarmé does not even do that. In a number of related ways he departs from everything familiar in his approach to the experience of art. First, he desires above all to avoid promoting the slightest relevance of any systematic approach to the experience. His thoughts on this subject have no method of their own which could make sense apart from concrete experiences. He simply presents the experiences in his own perspective. Similarly, he offers no judgments about art works. His "criticisms" of compositions (Wagner), paintings (Whistler, Manet), poems (Poe, Baudelaire, Rimbaud), dramas (Shakespeare), ballets and dances are designed to function as dialogues rather than as tribunals. Finally, Mallarmé does not even proffer reports to inform the public mind with outlines or details *of* the art works he peruses. He speaks *to* them more than *about* them. His thoughts on art are neither methodical, critical, nor descriptive in essence. Nor are they just poetical; they are too thoughtful for that. Whatever else they are, they represent an attempt to understand art in a radically new way.

In reviewing the approaches Mallarmé is intent upon avoiding, one can catch a suggestion of his positive intent. What he wants is a direct participation in the work of art. He expresses this want not as a program but as an embodiment. His own thoughts on art are essentially instances of taking part in the actual dynamics of the experience—instances accompanied by reflection, to be sure, but a style of reflection which moves with the work itself. The only other movement of his reflection is an occasional rejection of the various familiar styles which view art from the outside, as an object to be explained and explained away for reasons extraneous to the experience itself. It is his concern for the participation of man in art—and for man's experience of art in a way that emphasizes his necessary participation in it—that characterizes both Mallarmé's prose and poetry. Indeed, it is the concern of his, actively realized in his works, that puts him at the crossroads of a number of developments in French literary history; but that is not now the point.

Yet if participation is the positive intent of Mallarmé's writings, how can one account for his repeated comments that art somehow stands on its own two feet in implicit if not explicit defiance of man? Here we touch upon one of Mallarmé's points, albeit few in number about which there seems to be little doubt. Not only does his poetry seem to display an open indifference to the sensitivities of the reader but his prose also contains explicit statements of this indifference. For instance, in a piece originally entitled "*L'Action*" and later included in *Divagations* along with two other pieces under the heading "*Quant au livre,*" he writes: "Impersonified, a volume—inasmuch as the author removes himself from it—makes no claim to be approached by a reader" (M, 372). The work that issues from human efforts becomes independent of man. As it takes on form it withdraws from its creator; it governs its own meaning. Concomitant with its independence arises a suppression of the personality of the writer. In *"La Musique et les lettres,"* published the same year as *"L'Action,"* Mallarmé draws a comparison: "Literature, like hunger, consists in suppressing the Dear Sir who happens to write it" (M, 657). According to this formula, the consummation of writing, like the development of starvation, does not bring with it a completion of the man engaged in it, but rather his rejection. In emphasizing this possible aspect of the experience of art, Mallarmé is countering the ever recurrent and so inevitably prevalent tendency to understand artistic creations as extensions, expressions, or possessions of man. At times in perusing his writings, it seems that Mallarmé advocates an occult worshipping of a monstrous god who demands everything but gives nothing in return except possibly a leniency in his own indifference. It stands to reason, however, that if art is to present and govern its own meaning, man must be understood as first of all standing outside it, as first of all not being *with it,* as *not* participating in it. But then what becomes of the earlier claim that the unfamiliarity of Mallarmé's style is to be understood in terms of his intent to promote and embody movement along with the elements of art?

We would like to propose a way of understanding the two themes—the experience of art as participation and art as refusing participation—to complement one another in reality and to contradict one another only in appearances.

Most if not all art works do contain elements which invite participation. Something is generally recognizable in them, something is there with which we are familiar. Most artists find it nearly impossible to avoid relying upon some appeal to the common sensibilities of a possible set of people comprising an audience, a class of readers, spectators, or appreciators. Things are depicted from our everyday world, whether they be trees or tomatoes, in or out of context; familiar sensations are evoked, visual, auditory, or emotional; references are made, both intellectual and physical, to things like social ideals or sexual acts. Such invitations to participation are undeniable. The question is rather whether they are not ironical. Invitations to participate occur not for the reasons we ordinarily or initially think they do, not to confirm our interests in the recognizable things as we have come to conceive of them. They occur to change ordinary reality, to modify our interests so radically as to constitute an expulsion of everything but the fact of the interest itself and to substitute its own meaning in place of the meanings otherwise expected to develop. In concentrating upon the expulsion, Mallarmé seems to be advocating a new or different form of art; however, he is actually only noting what happens in the experience of art, contrasting his notes not with those of other men as artists, but with those of other men as critics. He is mainly *describing* what happens. Only by his placement of emphasis and importance is he *prescribing*, that is, influencing future developments in literary history.

In his essay *"Crise de vers"* (1886; slightly revised for *Divagations,* 1897), Mallarmé writes: "Every soul is a melody which must be renewed; and to this end each has his own flute or viola" (M, 363). Art calls into play instruments which each man already has; either that or it does not call anything at all into play. The experience of art always involves getting at the origin of things. This origin emerges as a melody, the melody peculiar to each man The melody is not anything in itself, though; left to itself, it dies It must be renewed. A man only is what he is, namely, his melody, insofar as he confronts the alien, something having the power to renew him: art. In the same way, it is the function of art to renew man. It is hardly anything in itself. It is what it is, the instigation of melody in confrontation with human beings. Art is essentially a work. The experience of art is the experience of art work, of emergence, of becoming. We become what we are to be in this experience. If we experience art, we do not simply take stock of an object presented to us, the mere result of art. We participate in a work. Only in this hyperbolic tension between the "I" and the "other" does the work emerge—and also the poles of the tension.

A dialectical experience is one in which elements first invite full participation. They then proceed to transform the interests of the invitation into another complex governing its own meaning and evoking the self of man and the presence of what he confronts out of the oblivion into which they otherwise sink. Art works are supremely dialectical in this sense. The crux of dialectic is a development taking as its basis what is initially given and relying on the internal conflict of forces for the generation of a situation of meaning transcending and yet incorporating this basis. A transcendence which still incorporates what is transcended is a radical transformation rather than just a new formation. In philosophical systems such those of Plato, Hegel, or Marx, dialectic refers to the development mainly in terms intellectual, historical, or social, respectively. In the experience of art, the development keeps its immediate and sensuous, and so aethetic, character by focusing attention on elements in our experience which can indeed be transformed, but not reduced to a category. Consequently, the development remains essentially momentary in time and transient in significance. We do not look to art for eternal truths, whether intellectual, historical, or social. We look to art—and art looks to us—for an experience of presence: here and now.

Experiencing the here and now requires a dialectical transformation of our patterns of perception simply because our immersion in the present ordinarily makes us oblivious to things. We do not ordinarily even see, hear, smell, taste, and touch what lies immediately before us, let alone take stock of our own position (self) in it. Whatever does lie before us requires revitalization through the renewal of the melody which we ourselves are, each in his own way. In a piece written for the inauguration of a monument to Théodore de Banville in the Jardin du Luxembourg (Paris) and published in 1892, Mallarmé puts the point clearly: *"The divine transposition, for the accomplishment of which man exists, proceeds from the fact to the ideal"* (M, 522). What lies before man as already done (fact) is not for that reason already completed (ideal). Man is the mediator of this completion (transposition). He is essentially one who participates creatively in the process of dialectical transformation, renewing the melody which is not only he, but his world.

The transposition Mallarmé accomplishes only in his poems, not in his epigrammatic comments on poetry. It does little good to consider the contents of *Divagations* except in juxtaposition to a consideration of his verse. Take his "Eventail de Madame Mallarmé" as an example (M, 57). He wrote several of these "fan" poems—over twenty—some of them actually on fans. This particular one was published in 1891, but originally written "in red ink on a silver-paper fan trimmed with white daisies" (M, 1475).

EVENTAIL

Avec comme pour langage
Rien qu'un battement aux cieux

Le futur vers se dégage
Du logis très précieux

Aile tout bas la courrière
Cet éventail si c'est lui
Le même par qui derrière
Toi quelque miroir a lui

Limpide (où va redescendre
Pourchassée en chaque grain
Un peu d'invisible cendre
Seule à me rendre chagrin)

Toujours tel il apparaisse
Entre tes mains sans paresse.

EVENTAIL

With for its language nothing
But a beat toward the heavens
Future verse detaches itself
From its precious abode.

Wing, very softly, messenger
This fan if it is one
The same through which behind
You a mirror has flashed

Limpid (where will redescend
Pursued in each grain
A bit of invisible ash
Enough to make me sorrow)

May it always thus appear
In your ever-moving hands.

The cardinal feature of the style of this poem is its evasiveness. It deliberately oscillates in its reference to an otherwise abstract idea and an obviously concrete thing. It intimates ideas about the enterprise of poetic effort as such, and yet its imagery derives from and returns to a tangible thing, namely, the fan and even the hands that hold it. To say that the experience of the poem is either that of the idea or that of the fan, or a mixture of the two, is to distort the actual language of the poem. Its language is rather that of the movement of oscillation itself. The idea *and* the fan are abstractions taken by themselves. One is not used as a metaphor for the other. To try to pin down the reference to a univocal direction of meaning would violate the experience of the poem. Its accomplishment is that it manages to say multiple things at once and that it unifies them, making each inextricable from the other. Each of the four stanzas and the poem as a whole embody this movement.

In the first stanza the ideational reference is the strongest. Future verse, we read, detaches itself from its patent origin with nothing but a beat upwards. Mallarmé's prevailing concern for language and the evolving futural orientation of the poetic enterprise, for a purified form of poetic articulation, comes into play in this apparent reference to a new form of verse. The reference is intellectual and prophetic and could be expressed and developed in a theoretical context better than in an aesthetic one. But notice that the emphasis of the statement falls on "Nothing but a beat . . . " The phrase, especially as it continues " . . . toward the heavens," connotes for the reader a sense of free flight, namely, that of the birds, and yet derives immediately from the contained movement of the fan. Thus the reference is already multidimensional. Furthermore, this kind of beat (that of a fan) has its significance not in itself, but in the air which it brings into motion. If there is a future verse, it is one whose movement is devoid of everything but what it immediately instigates. A fan moves a vital substance toward man. We know that already, but the stanza actually modifies the reference, since the movement is not directed toward the face of man, but toward the heavens. Thus the analogy is deliberately broken, and the power of the metaphor functions negatively as well as positively. The poem does not depict a number of similarities between future verse and fans. At best the one only suggests the others, since similarities as well as dissimilarities are evidenced. This is the art of poetic metaphor—to bring meanings together in tenuous, momentary, and mutually clarifying association. The experience of this association is essentially one of movement.

The second stanza locates the experience. The location is achieved, however, only through multiple ellipses. If we take it out of its poetic context and fill in the lacunas, we might reformulate the stanza thus: this fan, if it is (the right) one, (is such as a) wing, (and) gentle, (something like a woman) messenger—the same by which some mirror lights up behind you. Or, more likely, these four verses can be heard without any copula or simile, but simply as a vocative. In any event, we do not experience the unity of the stanza by means of reinstituting a grammar in this way. The unity is suggested more in the rhythm and the rhyme, without which the words would appear as a senseless chaos. The fan is mentioned in the second verse, but the indication of its presence is immediately qualified by an existential "if." Its gentleness—the soft, gliding movement we should associate with the function of a fan in a lady's hand—receives an allusion, but immediately in the same breath (literally), it is surrounded by two associated references, one to a wing and one to a messenger. And then it functions not to fan the face, but to bring something into play which is not ordinarily associated with fans: it affords the opportunity to a mirror—which the holder of the fan cannot even behold—for reflecting. All these associations are perfectly legitimate in their own right. It is only the manner of their juxtaposition which is fantastic. The purpose of the fantasy is hardly to induce us to enter into a dream-world, however. What happens is that in the presentation of the fan the very presence of it withdraws. We are left with a set of relations unified in appearance by a subject which tends to disappear. "The things themselves do exist," said Mallarmé in response to a question about naturalism during an interview published in 1891, "we don't have to create them; we only have to grasp their relations: these are the strings of relations which make up verses and orchestras" (M, 871). In the same interview he is recorded as saying: "To *name* an object is to suppress three-quarters of the joy of the poem; the joy consists in divining little by little: *suggest* it" (M, 869). And in a letter to Henri Cazalis in 1864, we read that his motto was: "To paint not the thing, but the effect that the thing produces."[33] The second stanza does just that: it is reference purified of the usual need to be based on the referent. The location of the experience is once again in the movement rather than in the goal.

The third stanza is the most enigmatic. It consists of one word standing alone, qualifying something not spelled out itself, and followed by a parenthetical remark (the parenthesis appears in the original fan but not in the first published version). Here we rely heavily upon the unity achieved through rhyme and rhythm. Something is limpid; there is no telling what exactly this something is. There is the "idea" suggested in the first stanza, and there is the "fan" indicated in the second stanza. Limpidity would apply best to something associated with light, and so the mirror mentioned in the previous stanza also becomes a candidate, but there is no reason to suppose that a short poem about a fan will devote a whole stanza to something coming up perhaps only incidentally in another stanza —unless the point is to suggest that in the functioning of a fan it is possible to discern a reflection of future verse. The reference in any event remains essentially ambiguous. Furthermore, the parenthetical remark throws no light on the referent, but speaks of a movement again presupposing it. The remark seems to be a reflection on the whole event described one-sidedly in each of the preceding stanzas: a little bit of invisible ash is going to float back down, pursued in each grain. Down from where? Apparently down from the heavens indicated in the first stanza. The ashes then seem to "stand for" the mortal remains of a poem which disintegrate, like a comet, in their heavenly and earthly course: the words now considered as *mere* words, dead and unevocative. And onto what? Apparently onto the earth, onto things, onto the fan, the hand, the mirror. The ashes, then, have a kinship with these things too. The movement is one of pursuit. Who pursues each grain of ash? Apparently the narrator himself. He moves too. And the movement is enough to cause him sorrow. The force of the stanza rests on this last verse. The kinds of things brought momentarily to light in the first two stanzas could be considered abstractly—in abstraction from necessary human involvement. But here the human involvement is accounted for: suggested again, not spelled out. Whenever man is required by nature to take part in a venture, the occasion is one of sorrow, no matter how much joy may issue from a successful completion of the requirement. One is first of all affected by the requirement, otherwise it presents no fundamental exigence.

The last stanza is brief and transparent. It consists of a simple and poignant exhortation that the fan, such as it has appeared in the experience of the poem, should so appear in your hands as you hold it. Notice that the poet could have *added* something at this point, say a moral or an explication of the metaphor. But he does not. He lets it stand: except that he throws it in the lap of man. He refuses to point to anything beside the fan and the fact that the holder is holding it. It is this worldly thing which continues to form the basis of the poetic experience, and so of creative effort. Even though the creative effort cuts itself off from the basis or, better, from reliance upon it, it has nothing *else* to rely on. The experience of art is here adumbrated: it is at once experience of the mysterious and experience of the secular. "At bottom," said Mallarmé in the interview of 1891, "the world is made to be consummated in a good book" (M, 872).

The entire poem lies inscribed on that of which it elusively speaks, on a fan. This in turn lies in the ever-moving hands of man. Moving along with the verses, the reader experiences a unity in the flow. This unity is forged by such factors as rhyme, rhythm, and the play of strophe, antistrophe, reflection, and climax (roughly, the four stanzas). But the arrangement of the elements (words with their images and mutual connotations) is initially foreign to the man who confronts it. So far the poem repels man. But if he is captured by the factors forging the aesthetic unity, a man fills in the lacunas and ellipses, becomes clear about the associations. This activity is not preparatory to his own movement—as though following the work were primarily a matter of being clever. The activity is not one of supplying missing verbs or solving riddles of connotative association. If we follow the poem, experience it as identical with what it says, we get along without explicitly supplying and solving. We get along on the basis of the congruence between our own activity and the movement comprising the poem. Our own activity is the "filler," not the verbs and lines of association.

In *"Eventail de Madame Mallarmé"* the pattern of activity and movement is established in terms of a marked elusiveness of ideas and things. The elusiveness ensures the dynamic character of the poem. The movement and activity do not cease as far as the poem is concerned. It does not provide for their termination; on the contrary, "May it always thus appear." The pattern makes no sense apart from the activity of following along within it. It is participative as well as repellent, human as well as inhuman.

In a piece on Wagner, written in 1885 and retouched for *Divagations* in 1897, Mallarmé remarked in prose-poem fashion: "Man and his authentic terrestrial sojourn, prove one another reciprocally / Thus, Mystery" (M, 545). Presumably, reflection on the experience of art contributes in its own way to this reciprocity.

rimbaud's departure

In the fifteenth century Pico della Mirandola tried to suggest the meaning of poetic writing by comparing a piece of literature to a ladder:

> Sometimes we descend, tearing the unity apart with a Titanic power and dispersing it into numerous fragments like the body of Osiris. At other times we ascend the ladder with the energy of a Phoebus who recollects these fragments, the limbs of Osiris, into a new unity.[34]

Such metaphorical imagery can be helpful and suggestive in that it induces us to think about the features of its object which might allow the expression to make sense. First, we would have to discover a certain duplexity featured in the poetic work, a duplexity permitting if not demanding two antithetical orientations toward it: that of dispersion and that of recollection. Next, we would have to understand the meaning of each of these antitheses separately, or how a poetic work actually effects disperson and recollection. Finally, we would have to come to terms with the simple fact that the expression claims a relevance for the gods: in what way would this process of descent and ascent warrant analogy with the divine?

These questions could not receive their due if we were merely to dwell upon Pico della Mirandola's metaphor as though it somehow contained its own meaning apart from its function of carrying us on into concrete instances of literature. What we need to do, then, is take up a particular example of poetic writing and see how the image of the ladder and alternate descensions and ascensions make sense in the actual situation.

We might turn to any poetic work since the metaphor makes a claim to general relevance. For various reasons, however, we will take the poetry of Arthur Rimbaud. A span of nearly five centuries separates it from Pico della Mirandola's original suggestion, and it would indeed be interesting if we could discover a recurrent element in that span of time. It is more important, though, that for a number of years the fashion in literary circles has been to underline one of the two antitheses as exhibited in Rimbaud's works: according to the figure, his works are descension, dispersions, and so require of us that we descend the ladder. Even a brief acquaintance with his poetry, not to mention his letters and general biography, lends a certain amount of plausibility to such telling categories of interpretation as "disorientation," "incoherence," "fragment," "dislocation," "anguish," and "alienation."

In a word, the import of Rimbaud's poetry often appears to be negative. Thus even the most generous interpreter finds himself embarrassed when faced with the question of what might be of positive interest; for we cannot immediately involve ourselves in what is merely negative, but must, like adolescents, quickly pass on to something else. It should then be singularly challenging to ask whether and how Rimbaud's works might provide for an ascension, for a unification—immediate appearances to the contrary notwithstanding. Is provision made in Rimbaud for climbing *up* the ladder?

We are prone to forget that any work, whether of poetic or of any other nature, argues at least implicitly for an ascension and for a unity—owing to the fact of its being *a* work. The view of utter dispersion and descension could not find expression without contradicting itself, since an expression must in principle lay claim to a unity of itself and to a validity of the issue it raises. There are many ways of achieving a self-consistency of viewpoint here. A common one is found at the level of a destitution which by its very nature allows of no direct or wrought productivity at all, let alone poetic creativity. However, as soon as one dares to raise characteristics of chaos and to place them in any sort of framework (a poem, a novel, an essay), one has introduced, produced, and presented order. The advent of order may not destroy the features of chaos, but neither does the chaos preclude the order. Thus it is, no doubt, that Rimbaud's work has irrevocably influenced and altered the course, and so the structure and order, of poetic expression in the French tradition. It would be unfair and shortsighted, then, to hold that only chaos prevails in his works. We must rather ask how it is that chaos and order, dispersion and unification, unstructure and structure each contribute to the peculiar character of Rimbaud's creations.

Any claim setting forth or proposing the peculiar nature of works of art or poetry must find its justification in the works themselves. Unlike a theoretical examination of a theoretical treatise, where the examination can rightly focus itself on a *tertium quid*, namely, the reality which the original treatise examines, the theoretical examination of a poetic or artistic work must speak directly to the "second thing," namely, the work itself, and only justify itself in these terms. The project of a critique is therefore laden with its own kind of difficulty: to reduce the subject to something else; to wrestle with the opponent in its own territory rather than to try to lure it into a land alien to it and familiar to us. Paradoxically enough, it seems that we can best decide whether a piece of literature is necessarily like a ladder allowing of ascension and descension if we do indeed climb it.

The poem *"Départ"* in *Les Illuminations* expresses the overriding character of Rimbaud's works, that of transition (R, 183).

DEPART

Assez vu. La vision s'est recontrée à tous les airs.
Assez eu. Rumeurs des villes, le soir, et au soleil et tourjours.
Assez connu. Les arrêts de la vie. — O Rumeurs et Visions!
Départ dans l'affection et le bruit neufs.

DEPARTURE

Seen enough. The vision was met with in every air.
Had enough. Sounds of cities, in the evening, and in the sun
  and always.
Known enough. Life's halts. — O Sounds and Visions!
Departure in new affection and new noise.

What sort of duplexity does this poem evidence? What is the character of each element of the duplexity? What justification might there be for finding an analogy with the divine? In approaching the poem with these questions in mind we might recall a comment which Rimbaud is said to have made when his mother asked him about the meaning of *Une Saison en enfer*: "I want to say what it says, literally, and with all its meanings" (R, 656).

"*Départ*" comprises four verses. The first three seem to stand together and constitute a statement of the experience of "having had enough," while the last verse sets down what seems to be a change from the first three, the experience of "taking leave." Thus we seem to have a "ladder" of sorts: the poem reveals a difference between beginning and end, and its whole sense and mood arise because of a solicited movement from the one to the other. The poem makes no sense at all unless it succeeds in invoking the mood of "having had enough" and so of being driven out of the realm described by the first three verses into another realm, one intimated only by the ambivalent terms "affection" and "new sounds."

Before embarking on a detailed exploration of each line of the poem to understand whether and how it succeeds in invoking the sense of movement, we might ask more precisely about the character of these four verses which would seem to allow a viable duplexity in the movement. After all, it is a simple and even boring matter to remark on the tiresomeness of one's situation and the need to move out into something else. Such a remark is characteristic of our most ordinary experiences; we do not even have to become reflective to any appreciable measure, let alone poetic, to be satiated and to desire a departure. Does Rimbaud's poem mean to present and repeat the humdrum?

A rudimentary requirement for a duplexity in the experience of movement is that the beginning and the end somehow belong to each other. If a poem were to suggest a straightforward movement lacking all ambivalence, it would belong in the same genus if not the same species as signposts along the road, the function of which is to allow us to forget them for the sake of the direction or instruction they indicate. If a linguistic work cannot embody a movement, it can hardly be called poetic; it must rather be considered instrumental.

A second look at "*Départ*" shows a peculiar facet of its structure: the third verse, introduced by the sentiment "known enough," appears to add just one more case of tiresomeness, but is actually a reflection on the first two verses. This reflection is evidenced in the statement that what is known is first and foremost "Life's halts," that is, a general impasse such as the first two verses describe in the imagery of seeing and hearing. However, the third verse is more than a general summation of what has preceded. It goes on, after the pause indicated by the dash, to express a nostalgic lament: "O Sounds and Visions!" Because of this lament, we are carried into a movement having an end in view—already in the third verse: sounds and visions are not denounced, they are sought after. The fourth verse elaborates this search, but it does not introduce the search. The direction of movement is already postulated in the consummated expression "enough!"; that is to say, what is demanded is a modification of sounds and visions—such that they become truly what they are.

All by itself, or apart from the lament expressed in the third verse, the fourth would invoke a simple linear movement asking us to forget one thing and take up another; it would be a typical and therefore uninteresting exhortation, a "ladder" which would only allow descent, that is, the dispersion of the elements of experience, and would defy ascent, that is, the preservation and unification.

"*Départ*" is essentially duplex. According to Pico della Mirandola's metaphor, it allows two different orientations: it can carry us downward and it can carry us upward; it can tune in both to the need for disbanding and scattering the elements of experience and to the need for maintaining and recollecting them. But this is only the beginning. We must now ask whether and how the poem not only presents the need but also fortifies it, substantiates it, and maybe even fulfills it, rather than leave it in the form of a bald statement. In other words, how are the movements of dispersion and unification, each separately, brought to light in "*Départ*"? To answer this question we will turn to the poem itself.

I

Seen enough. The vision was met with in every air.

The usual, and even traditional, means of attaining insight and understanding is vision. Human projects can generally be defined in terms of coming to see something, that is, knowing it by overcoming the blindness of ignorance. However, this verse invokes not another and different project, but an opposition to the ordinary, vulgar, and intellectual one: enough has been seen. Something of an explanation of this reversal follows in the same verse: Vision has found itself, has met up with itself in all "airs," that is, in all places, their tones and their looks. The ambiguity of this statement must be deliberate. Since the drift of the whole poem is initially one of impasse, we can safely assume that the expression "having found itself, met up with itself" *(s'est rencontrée)* is meant to invoke the sense of "running up against itself" and "getting in its own pathway" instead of confronting what is seen proper. Vision is turned back upon itself no matter where it turns. We become self-conscious to the point of losing consciousness of the rest of the world.

The imagery of the verse embodies what it says. The impasse of vision is not only stated as a proposition which would need to be verified in some extraneous way; it is expressed and verified by the reference to its locale: *"les airs"* carries a sense not primarily visual but relevant to the several senses notably that of touch (the *feel* of the atmosphere, of a place), that of hearing (the *tone),* and finally that of sight (the *countenance).* If the poet was not intending to play up this ambiguity, he might just as well have been more explicit and said instead "the *objects,*" "the *colors,*" or "the *forms,*" any of which would have maintained a clear reference to seeing. But he did not, and this is perhaps not astonishing, for the problem and impasse are precisely this: Vision has lost its object, flounders in itself. Under such conditions we do not withdraw ourselves from our various senses; instead we find ourselves overcome by the confusion resulting from our inability to focus appropriate attention on anything in particular.

II

Had enough. Sounds of cities, in the evening, and in the sun and always.

Once again, we must take note of the ordinary tendency to work toward an end in view, defined humanly as coming to have something which one did not have before. But here we have the statement that enough has been had, the drive for possession is somehow abnegated. What is to be had from the cities, in the evening, under the sun, at any time—all this fails to suffice. We are not told what it is that fails to find its adequation; that is, we do not hear what these things do not suffice for. This lack of information must be understood as essential to the sense of the verse if it is taken to convey a radical experience of lack. The statement of having had enough is not meant to preface a list of all things that are had, a list which might in turn form a propaedeutic to understanding something specific which could be added to the list. Just as the experience of having *seen* enough is one in which we are concerned with quality rather than with quantity, the experience of having *had* enough is one which already takes us and our concerns on to an entirely different plane. The poem underlines further this radical shift of orientation in the latter portion of the verse purporting to explain the experience: Instead of going on to enumerate either what is had (fame, knowledge, or power) in a Faustian fashion, or what needs to be had (insight, feeling, death, etc.) and thereby invoking the need to verify these enumerations, the verse simply mentions the "sounds of cities, in the evening, and in the sun and always." In other words, what is evident on the occasion of the experience of "having had enough" is the way things speak to one when they are experienced as possessions: They speak monotonously at all times, as the verse suggests by its claim to exhaustiveness.

The choice of the term *"rumeurs"* is telling. It can mean "what is heard" as well as "what is going on in general." Although the term *"rumeurs"* seems odd in view of the statement about "having," it fits directly in with the choice of *"les airs"* in the first verse. Both terms have ambiguous referents, thereby invoking a rudimentary confusion of the senses, a sort of *disordering of all the senses,* which Rimbaud aspires to in *"Les Lettres du voyant"* (R, 268-270). *"Les airs"* and *"les rumeurs"* both entail the sense of sound without excluding references broader in scope. Indeed, the whole poem, when experienced in its fluency, would suggest that they belong together, since the explanation contained in the first verse is a complete sentence ending in *"les airs,"* while the explanation contained in the second verse, starting straight off with *"rumeurs,"* is but a fragment, as though it were continuing the thought of the first verse.

III

Known enough. Life's halts.—O Sound and Visions!

In this third verse we notice for the third time a simple re-versal of our habitual and for that reason generally implicit mode of concern. Enough is known: that is, the problem is no longer one of knowledge. The explanation of this experience seems to be simp-ly that what knowledge is directed toward, essentially "Life's halts." Ordinarily we would assume that it was the nature of knowledge to allow us to achieve a certain fluency of movement.

We have noted that the experience invoked at this junction of knowledge precipitates immediately into a lament, into a reflec-tion on the previous two junctures:" — O Sounds and Visions!" While enough is known and while there is no suggestion that there might be any alternative knowledge, hearing and seeing hold out some hope or at least some desire for revival. Thus Rimbaud can speak of arriving at, not knowing, the unknown ("It is a question of arriving at the unknown through a disordering of *all the senses*"), and of becoming a seer (R, 268-70).

The structure of these first three lines is tightly woven. Al-though all three begin by introducing some experience of "having enough," they are wrapped together by the fact that only the first verse constitutes a full sentence, while the latter two differ from the first by being literally dependent clauses, thoughts appending the first one. The last verse differs from the first in being a reflec-tion on all that went before. Finally, although structurally self-contained in that they provoke at the end a return to the beginning, these lines suggest a movement, albeit a movement not defined by the advent of knowledge. As self-contained, they do not finish the matter, but precisely set the condition and necessitation for motion. The fundamental experience of self-contained movement, as op-posed to simple rest and static experience, is capped off by the final verse of the poem.

IV

Departure in new affection and new noise.

In order to discover and return to the meaning of that which has apparently lost its meaning, it becomes necessary to "take leave."

What could this mean? Would it not be more to the point to "enter" into something rather than "depart" into it? The poet is evidently introducing or rather sustaining a deliberate ambiguity in the movement. Given the experience of the need for "sounds and visions," a need essentially correlative to the experience of "having enough" of the sorts of sounds and visions to be had, particularly as they function with regard to their traditional subsumption under the rubric of knowledge—given all this, a certain *departure* would be more fundamental to the aspiration of attaining "new affection and new sound" than a straightforward *entrance*. Why? A brief reflection on the problem of development in general might help us in answering this question.

Poetic expression brings something fundamental to the fore. Since poetry is not suitable for the philosophical exposition of fundamental *features* of reality which would, belonging to reality, go beyond the expression itself, poetic expression must comprise a fundamental *experience* of reality, one that is self-contained in some way. As bespeaking experiences rather than features, a poem must embody a movement taking its bearings from reality, in either a positive or a negative way (as attraction or repulsion, it makes no difference at the outset). This movement, in order to constitute an experience, must be one that comes to something: it must be a development. We do not, properly speaking, have *an* experience, and so we cannot have *a* poem, without a sustaining development: If nothing happens, our attention goes on to something else, that is, our attention must move in any event, and experience is always kinesthetic in one fashion or another. And if, contrary to some Cartesian views of human destiny, we necessarily begin with something, the enduring problem lies in getting away from that initial level, and only secondarily in attaining to another level. Whereas the traditional philosophic view has always been one of entering into reality, the poetic "problem" lies in the fact that we are already in a reality of sorts—or in an illusion, if we would rather call it that. And if there will be any development, it will be conditioned by a prior breaking-away. Similarly Oedipus' whole problem lies in realizing and overcoming precisely that which he himself is, or was and now must forever be, rather than in achieving a vantage point from which to view an eternal verity.

The "departure" singularly embodied in Rimbaud's poem has for its only point of reference new affection and new sound. According to the inherent ambiguity of the preposition, the departure can be as much within, thus conditioned by these new regions, as directed into or toward them. The emphasis on the "new" would, however, suggest that what is at stake in the departure is a revelation of some sort. There is in any event a singular lack of a clear statement of what is to be revealed: merely new affection and new sound. The ambiguity is compounded by the fact that the brevity of the reference allows us to interpret even these words in two different ways. On the one hand, *"affection"* can be taken either in the classical sense of "reception" or in the more popular sense of "emotion." On the other hand, *"bruits"* can suggest something more neutral like "sound" or something more pejorative like "noise." The general tenor of the poem makes these ambiguities appear absolutely essential: enough has been seen, had, and known; what is seen, had, and known cannot contribute to a definition of what needs to be revealed; they only define the need for revelation. To be thoroughly consistent with the purport of this experience, we must agree that the departure, the development, shall not have any specific goal outlined in advance. What we are after is not just something different (something defined by the way it differs from what has already been seen, had, and known), but something new.

Meanwhile, the development embodied in the fluency of the poem as a whole suggests a further connection between the ambiguity of the last line and the statements of the previous lines. This connection serves to alleviate the tendency of the ambiguity to become a mere emptiness. While the fourth verse indicates some sort of development of "new affection and new sound," the previous lines lamented the situation of seeing (visions) and having (sounds). Is there meant to be a parallel here, or is it merely a coincidence that there are, on the one hand, basically two modes of the old and worn-out and, on the other hand, two modes of departure into the new? It is impossible to experience fully the poem without noting the association of the old voices and the new sounds. Further reflection recalls to mind that vision is tightly bound up with what one meets up with, the way one is affected; a seeing without full-bodied "affection," that is both reception and feeling, is empty: it just meets up with itself, and enough of that has been seen. The fact still remains, though, that two different words with wholly different connotations (apart from their identical denotations) emerge at the end. Is this shift in terminology a mere ruse, a cleverness or—once again—a meaningless coincidence blown up by the over-indulgent critical mind?

The dominant tone of *"Départ"* bespeaks a movement toward the new at the expense of the old. In the imagery of Pico della Mirandola, we might say that the poem most readily provides the opportunity if not the necessity for a descension, a destruction of the old accompanied by a mere intimation of the new: an intimation, not a construction or even a projection. But precisely because no specific content is outlined in advance, and because the old content is forcefully and poetically pointed up as inadequate, the intimation is one of the *radically* new. And the words employed to describe the radically new must likewise be radically new—not in the sense that they would be inventions, but rather that they would depart from our ordinary expectations: the departure cannot rightly be one into new visions and new voices, but it might be one into new affections and new sounds.

This last argument touches upon a complex subject: the appropriate mode of poetic expression. It is unfortunate indeed when we are on the lookout for some universal standard to which all poetic expression might hopefully measure up. Poetry is poetry because its mode of expression aims to coincide with what it wants to say. It follows then, if what it wants to say is always something unique, particular, and singular, that its mode of expression will always be unique, particular, and singular—anything but universal. Or if it is universal, it will be such because the unique, particular, and singular are after all what is most universally important and appealing to the mind of man. But this latter kind of universality must be distinguished from that of any kind of standard by which the work of art could be measured. There is something to the saying that the work produces its own standard, that it creates the universality, rather than measures up to a preconceived one.

If *"Départ"* had ended up in some such statement as "entrance into new sounds and new voices," it would have indeed provoked an experience of the new. The new however would have been more of the same, more of what one has had enough already. If such movement were the purport of the poem, its brevity and conciseness would have been unforgivable, since it might well have gone on to produce a catalogue of the old to be employed as an index of the new. As the poem stands, however, it evidently enjoys its whole meaning as a provocation of movement into the radically new, into what serves both to undermine and to substitute the old "sounds and visions." Thus the shift into the new terminology peculiar to the fourth verse, into terms largely alien to the general drift of the preceding verses and yet akin enough to suggest a relation, is itself an embodiment of the movement of which the poem speaks; the form and the content aim to coincide: it is poetic expression.

So, looking back upon the whole poem in its fluency, we might well ask: what is peculiar about its poetic expression? First of all, it cannot be denied that Pico della Mirandola's metaphor somehow applies to this instance of poetic writing: *"Départ"* allows of both the experience of unification and that of dispersion—dispersion by its rhythmic and paradoxical rejection of what is seen, had, and known, and unification by the experience of the paradox of departure and return becoming increasingly apparent in the movement of the poem from the beginning to the end. Meanwhile, however, what is most remarkable is the manner in which this two-fold experience is induced. Traditionally the work of art has generally tended to portray some sort of problematic relationship between a beginning and an end which tended to bring about a movement from the one to the other such that both were preserved, the movement being self-contained and therefore particularly rich as an experience of possibilities. But Rimbaud's work deviates from the tradition in a fundamental and definitive way. Instead of portraying a confusion at the beginning (witness Sophocles' *Oedipus,* Shakespeare's *Hamlet,* or Goethe's *Faust)* in a manner devoted to bringing about a movement toward a resolution, *"Départ"* portrays an inadequacy at the start, an inadequacy which is more akin to order than confusion (enough of what has already been seen, had, and known—that is, ordered). Then the poem proceeds to bring about a movement toward a departure, which is more akin to confusion than to resolution. What is patently peculiar in this mode of poetic expression is that the end is a statement and an embodiment of the radically new and only from here on out retroactive on the old (the lament). While traditional modes of expression were evidently anchored in unification, we witness here a mode anchored in dispersion: departure.

Taking leave of the poem proper, we must ask what might be at stake in this deviation from the tradition. After all, mere opposition to tradition often comes down to a sham fight in which one dares not really defeat the opponent, since one derives one's substance and direction from him by a simple process of inversion. In order to appreciate a departure from tradition, we must be able to perceive what it is that the departure holds out, not what it opposes. Our poem *states* in this regard nothing but "new affections and new sounds," a statement which is not terribly helpful by itself. The poem as a whole, however, embodies a complex movement which far surpasses any propositional statements also contained therein, a movement which contains itself and thereby fulfills the necessary, albeit formal condition for poetic expression. How is this telling "embodiment" actually effected?

Poetic expression comes forth as language. A simple observation, but one that often goes unnoticed because of the prevalence of language at the level of ordinary experience, a level which hardly comes to well-rounded expression and so tends to cover up its linguistic character. It follows then that the particular embodiment of movement by a poem will be effected by its mode of language or linguistic expression. It is in language that we must look for the answer to our question.

A possible misunderstanding must be avoided at the outset. When we recognize that poetry is language, we do not by that fact commit ourselves to any view which construes language as a thing in the world alongside other things, for example, as a structural pattern of human behavior amenable to the techniques of the social scientist or the semanticist. Before language can be so construed (and it no doubt can be so construed and considered for some practical purposes), it functions as a fundamental event in which the world itself, rather than a set of empirical structures, comes into being for man, either clearly or obscurely. If poetry is to enjoy any prominence in the life of man, it must be rooted in some such event. The particular character of any given poem would, accordingly, stand in relation to this autochthony. How are we to gain an intimation of language, if not an understanding, in this work of Rimbaud's?

We can turn to the poet himself. In May 1871 Rimbaud wrote two letters, one to Georges Izambard and one to Paul Demeny (R, 267-274). They describe what it means to engage in the enterprise of poetry—at least in Rimbaud's opinion. A consideration of this radical description might pave the way to a better understanding of Rimbaud and the influence he has had on subsequent writers. There are two observations in these letters to which we will give consideration. The first reads:

It's a question of coming to the unknown by a disordering of *all the senses.*

A few days later Rimbaud reformulates this statement: "The Poet makes himself into a *visionary* by a long, arduous and calculated *disordering* of *all the senses.*" The poet is attempting to express his conception of the "event" (of what it is that most fundamentally must come to the fore) in terms of a confrontation with the unknown (rather than conversion of the unknown into something known), a confrontation which must be preceded by an overcoming of the ordinary patterns of perception. But why this necessary precondition? Because, we are told further on, it is only by going through, and so in some sense beyond, *all* possible combinations of sensation that one is in a position to extract the "quintessences": "Every form of love, of suffering, of madness; he searches himself, he consumes all the poisons in him, keeping only their quintessences." This extraction must be a violation, since there is already order; traditionally, the institution of insight was not primarily a matter of violation because violation is a breaking up of order, while insight was understood as directed precisely toward order. Thus it is in ancient myth and poetry rather than in traditional philosophy that Rimbaud finds his counterpart: "Therefore the poet is truly a stealer of fire. He is charged with humanity, even the *animals;* he must make his inventions smelt, felt and heard; if what he brings back from *down there* has form, he gives it form, if it is unform, he gives it unform. A language must be found;—Moreover, all speech being an idea, the time of a universal language will come!"

What is the basic meaning and purport of these strange statements? One thing is evident. Confrontation with reality is not understood in the traditional way of bidding us to put our senses in order and thereby realize the order of reality. On the contrary, we are told that the senses are to be systematically *dis*ordered. This disordering, moreover, is to be accomplished by the poet according to a new understanding, or at least an intimation, of the possibilities and necessities of language. Thus throughout Rimbaud's works we witness a violation of sense-images, a deliberate confusion of the senses. We recall for instance that the first verse of *"Départ,"* when speaking of seeing, invoked the ambiguous image of *"les airs,"* while the second verse spoke of places, light and dark, when talking about hearing—and the ideal of knowledge is completely set aside in favor of a sensuous confrontation of the essentially unknown. But it must be borne in mind that these strange reversals would probably go unnoticed if it were not for the general impetus of the work, which carries us beyond the ordinary into the open-ended departure.

Is Rimbaud's project here just a matter of caprice to be explained simply as a preference or a taste on his part? Whenever we try to rely on "matters of taste," we are implicitly upholding a view in which only the solipsistic individual, affirming merely himself and using the rest of the world to express himself, counts. Is this consequence compatible with Rimbaud's entire view, then? We can hardly answer in the affirmative when we recall his remark that the disordering was "long, arduous and calculated." Moreover, the poet is "charged" with the whole world, and he must extract the "quintessences." Far from wishing to enjoy a merely "subjective" experience and thereby to affirm the primacy of the self over the world, Rimbaud seems to be suggesting that what is primary is precisely the world over the self. If the senses are to be disordered, it is not because this is man's delight ("the sufferings are enormous"), but because it is man's destruction—for the sake of the world: "He comes to the unknown and when, driven to madness, he finishes by losing the intelligibility of his visions, he has still seen them! Let him be destroyed in his leap by those unnamable, unutterable and innumerable things: there will come other horrible workers: they will begin at the horizons where he has succumbed." This primacy of the world and vision over the self and its knowledge becomes explicitly stated in the second observation:

> It is wrong to say: I think. One should say:
> I am thought.

This statement occurs in the context of the previous one, and is made in anticipation of the charge that it might be his "fault" that he understands himself to be a poet: this understanding does not issue from him at all, and so the traditional metaphysical proposition "I think" must be reversed to read something like "I am thought," that is, I *am* only as a reflection of the world. Thus Rimbaud can go on to say that "*I* is another" and that, to speak figuratively, it is not the business of the wood to lay claim to being the violin, just as it cannot be laid at the doorstep of the brass that it is actually a trumpet: "So much the worse for the wood that discovers it's a violin, and to hell with the heedless who cavil about something they know nothing about! . . . If brass wakes up as a trumpet, it isn't to blame. To me this is evident: I witness the birth of my thought: I look at it, I listen to it: I give a stroke of the bow: the symphony begins to stir in the depths or comes bursting onto the stage." The point is clear enough as far as it goes. Rimbaud expresses a fundamental concern about the priority of end over means, and the self of man is put down to a means, while the smelt, felt, and heard world is put down as the end. This reversal apparently constitutes a rebuttal for the Romantics who somehow failed to achieve the greatness of the Greeks even though they took up the issue of the place of man: "If the old imbeciles had not found only the false significance of the Ego, we would not have to be sweeping away these millions of skeletons which, since time immemorial, have been accumulating the products of those cockeyed intellects claiming themselves to be the authors."

We noticed that in *"Départ"* there is brought to the fore a radical experience of recognition and departure, an experience which is human in the strongest sense of the word. And yet the "humanity" of the poem comes into view as a paradox. The recognition and departure are not rooted in the "ego," the "I" of experience; these are one and all rooted in the world itself. The systematic eliminations of the narrator as one who can rightly bring the experience to the fore as *his* or as some ego's experience are only a part of the view upholding the new conception of the revelatory event peculiar to poetic language. But it is a part which dominates the character of Rimbaud's poems. It is said that Banville remarked, after reading *"Le Bâteau ivre"* that the poem was fine . . . except that it should have been prefaced by a verse running something like "I am a boat." Rimbaud demurred. In *"Départ"* it is not "I" who has had enough of the world; it is "I" who has had enough of the "I," of what only comes back to oneself: "The vision was met with in every air." What is needed is an overcoming of the "I" for the sake of the world: a departure into it.

We have been considering a new instance of creation, which is not new in the sense in which all creation brings forth either the new or a new view of the old, but one that is new because it is something of a reflection on a different conception of creation. New affection and new sounds are accomplished by departure rather than appointment, a departure in which it is relevant to arrive but not to know. *"Départ"* seems to bid one to be open to the experience of a new way in which the things of the world might speak to one. The bidding is not propositional, however; it is poetic. This means that the poem not only indicates but also embodies the experience in its language. A new conception of creation entails a new conception of language. But whatever begins anew must be allowed to speak for itself. Thus, language can only be universal when things are allowed to speak for themselves and men are willing to listen rather than to assert and insert their own egos into the issue. We might then redo Rimbaud and say:

> It is wrong to say: I speak. One should say:
> I am spoken.

The experience of *"Départ"* is the experience of creation, a revelation of and confrontation with the world. That such an experience is initially one of "departure" makes sense because the formation of the new requires the dissolution of the old. Thus we have unwittingly answered our third question about the applicability of Pico della Mirandola's metaphor to Rimbaud's poem: The event of creation warrants reference to the gods and here it particularly warrants reference to Phoebus, the Egyptian god of the underworld, since the creation depicts the primacy of the world to the sacrifice of the self.

rimbaud and the experience of art

"Human labor! this is the explosion that lights up my abyss from time to time" (R, 241). With these words the prose poem *"L'Eclair"* begins in Rimbaud's *Une Saison en enfer.* They are enigmatic words in an enigmatic poem. For our attention is drawn to the domain of human labor as providing an opportunity for enlightenment, first of all the enlightenment of the narrator of the work and then possibly that of the reader who consents to attend to the domain. And yet the body of the prose poem comprises a review of the sorry elements of the human experience of labor. From a hospital bed the narrator, apparently moribund, recalls with a certain amount of irony the modern reversal of Ecclesiastes: the view that human enterprise, far from being vain, is progress. He, the narrator, will confront his own duty by setting this duty aside. Human labor is too easy a solution to satisfy his pride: resistance to death cannot have for him the meaning of a desire to return to daily routine and obligation.

The domain of human labor has its own manifold of meanings and is functional by virtue of them. But the manifold of various meanings does not necessarily and autonomously configure itself into a meaningful whole. On the contrary, the habitual repetition of patterns of behavior dazes and dulls one, the unbending demands for strenuous exertion and attention engulf one, and the constant anticipation of recurrent and increasing reward consumes one. In 1871 Rimbaud wrote to Izambard that he would never work, that he was on strike (R, 268), and a year later he wrote to Verlaine, "Labor is farther removed from me than my fingernail from my eye" (R, 283).

At the time Rimbaud wrote and lived, the industrial revolution was at its torturous peak. The significance of this revolution for us today is multi-dimensional, but one thing can be said in the context of Rimbaud's concerns: there was installed on earth and instilled in the spirit of men an assumed primacy of immanence. The principle arose that human experience was to become meaning-*ful* by way of the various meanings engendered in the fulfillment of tasks pertaining to the elemental livelihood of both individual and state. The interrelated views of the aristocracy and the clergy, which held to a human destiny that transcended the realm of material existence, were losing their hold at the level of European man's most concrete concerns. Karl Marx had attempted to formulate the way human labor could configure itself into a meaningful whole for man through the dialectical development of industry. Nietzsche remarked somewhat later that, although labor was beginning to detract from religion and take its place, it could not hope to configure itself into a meaningful whole since labor served precisely to stupify man in the face of manifest meaninglessness.[35]

Rimbaud's poem refers to human labor as an explosion bringing forth a light revealing an abyss—the abyss of the narrator and possibly that of the reader. As an explosion, the character of human labor is that of instability: labor may stand or fall. Precisely in its instability, though, labor points up something about what it means to be human: the explosive nature of human labor dissipates the darkness and reveals the depths and dangers of man's relationship with his world. Human labor is the context of possible development, the framework of a drama in which human experience may— or may not—be consummated. Human labor provides each man with a definition of what it is that is to become meaningful. As such, though, it does not itself set the standard of meaningfulness.

It is *art* which sets the standard of meaning. Art may serve many different purposes and it can have a wide variety of incidental functions within human experience. Art objects can contain elements drawn from cultural settings and thus provide material for historical or anthropological interests. They can accumulate social prestige and monetary value, snob appeal and/or educational import. They can also occasion sentimental reminiscence and even total emotional submission. But aside from all that, art may function within a broader scope of experience; it refashions human experience as a whole into the image of a standard. Perhaps there are other modes of human activity, politics and philosophy at their best, for example, that also set a standard for human experience as a whole. These other modes are exclusive; they require special aptitudes and inevitably the added ability to cope with the conflicts that arise from competition. Art, however, is inclusive: it presents directly, that is, aesthetically, models of meanings that converge into meaningfulness. In other words, art is made of immediacy which points the way toward the consummation of human activity in its intuitive spontaneity. And such human activity is neither primarily emotional nor primarily intellectual: it is simply human labor.

How, exactly, does Rimbaud's own work contribute to the standardization of meaning for human experience, to the consummation of human involvement with things? The theorist must ask this question of Rimbaud's poetry. Yet from Rimbaud himself he will receive no direct answer. For this poet, unlike many others in the last two centuries, conspicuously renounced theoretical expatiations upon his poetry. He was not a theorist in the manner, say, of his predecessor Baudelaire. But this absence of theory hardly bespeaks a lack. Rather, it indicates something about the standpoint of Rimbaud's work which takes a position in the thick of human activity in its immediacy and manifests its development at this point. Thus it is that the experiences evoked in Rimbaud's poems defy passive admiration or docile appreciation. They require that one assume the position of the artist (poet) himself. The theorist can, then, extract an answer by indirect means, by asking about the artist's position. For Rimbaud contributes to the standard of meaning by creating articulations which place the reader in the predicament of the creative process itself. The reader cannot begin with an appreciation of outward form; he must rather plunge into a participation in the inner creation.

These reflections have to be supported by a direct analysis of the poet's work. But first we must do what Rimbaud does not do: recall the formal nature of the creative process, if only in a rough and general outline so that we may better perceive how Rimbaud changes it to suit his special purposes.

The creative process is one incorporating various disparate elements into a whole. A variety of meanings, more or less familiar and recognizable, are integrated to allow for an experience which is both unique and unified. Since the elemental meanings are derived from the domain of the familiar and recognizable, one of the tasks facing the artist is to dislodge them from their customary abode. Thus the relocation of a familiar meaning into the work of art brings with it a sensation of strangeness, newness, or uniqueness which in turn occasions the focusing of attention necessary for the experience of art. The result—a poem, a painting, or whatever—is a tense synthesis of what might otherwise disintegrate from internal contradiction: what we might call formed chaos or chaotic formation.

The creative process shares with any human labor—and therefore the artist with any artisan—one basic dimension of its pervasive structures. Any human labor, any human activity or enterprise, proceeds by the selection of available materials to the end of constructing and maintaining a coherent whole. Even today's semiskilled factory worker, on an assembly line and repeatedly performing a limited and yet more or less exacting task, must exercise attention with regard to the variation in detail, acknowledge if not know the larger scope of operations, and accept his responsibility to uphold the whole by fulfilling his own part. It would be difficult to produce an example of a truly human labor which lacked the basic structure of discrimination and construction, although it may not be at all difficult to discern examples of human failure in this regard. By the same token, experience of chaos is also present in any truly human labor, perhaps less dramatically than in the work of the artist. Viewed from the outside, by the consumer, the production of an artifact may seem to be a purely mechanical matter. But viewed from the inside, from the standpoint of actually doing and undergoing the labor, the course of production threatens at every moment to present the laborer or artisan with an upsurge of undetermined detail. Do what we may to ensure a total predetermination in the daily routine of exertion and flow of materials, the very fact of doing something entails the need to confront and incorporate unforeseen elements. Thus two different failures are generally recognized: that of failing really to do something, that is, to confront alien materials, and that of failing to cope with materials in their unforeseeable variety.

To be human is to share in some way in the creative process, and to be an artist or a poet is to take a stand in the creative process in a way bringing the human share in it to light. Conclusions of this nature have often been asserted, and the arguments

called in to support them have been various. One example ante-
dating Rimbaud by nearly a century is the argument of J. G.
Herder (1744-1803). For him language is the expression of human
reflection. By selecting distinguishing marks of things out of the
"vast ocean of sensations," that is, out of the chaos he confronts,
man exercises his reflective nature.[36] Herder thus interprets the
adage that poetry is more primordial than prose by noting that the
peculiar and universal character of the human being is reflection
manifested in language. Herder feels that the very essence of
poetry entails a simultaneous expression of the human soul (in
mythology) and the nature it confronts (in epic).[37] This kind of
argument has undergone a wide variety of apparently conflicting
formulations in the modern era, but the basic point has remained
the same: that man, by virtue of his very humanity and by nothing else, can make sense out of his work through his own activity
of configuration, that every man is basically his own poet, although
his poetry may be stale and trite.

Igor Stravinsky stresses the kinship between artist and artisan when he speaks of the creative process, exemplified in his
own vocation as an "inventor of music." The common trait uniting
the two is performance: the experience of art from the artist's
standpoint is one of actually doing something, not just coming up
with something at the end of the process:

> The word "artist," as it is most generally understood
> today to bestow on its bearer . . . the privilege of being
> accepted as a pure mind . . . is entirely incompatible
> with the role of the *homo faber*.

> The very act of putting my work on paper—of, as
> we say, kneading the dough is inseparable from the
> pleasure of creation. So far as I am concerned, I
> cannot separate the spiritual effort from the psycho-
> logical and physical effort; they confront me on the
> same level and do not present a hierarchy.

> The idea of work to be done is for me so closely
> bound up with the idea of arranging materials and
> of the pleasure afforded by the actual doing of the
> work that, should the impossible happen and my work

be suddenly given to me in a perfectly completed
form, I should be embarrassed and nonplussed by it,
as by a hoax.

In the same context we read that, "whatever field of endeavor
has fallen to our lot, even if it is true that we are *intellectuals,* we
are called upon not just to cogitate, but to perform." Stravinsky
affirms the place of the creative process at the heart of man's nature. For him, artistic activity is but an explicit form of human
activity as such.[38]

While much can be learned from pondering the words
of such thinkers and artists as Herder and Stravinsky, it is necessary to interpose a dissenting comment. The artist must do what the
artisan cannot do. The artist realizes in his work a configuration
of materials in such a manner that the various and disparate meanings of these materials converge to form a confine of experience
both unified and meaningful. The artist produces a work which
draws a variety of meanings into itself, while the artisan produces
an artifact which leads out in various directions into the world of
use. The artist fits things into a work, while the artisan fits his
artifact into other things. The artist creates his own unity, while
the artisan produces an element within a larger unity which he
does not define but rather acknowledges. The artist allows for an
experience of meaningfulness, while the artisan sees to it that what
he does has a meaning. Both gather up materials and so account
for manifolds of meanings in the process of human labor, but the
artist standardizes what the artisan simply undertakes and under-
goes. Although the two are linked by the common domain of their
labors, the experience of art and that of labor invite contrary standpoints. Perhaps every man is called upon to assume both standpoints
in all their contrariness, but he initially and abidingly takes his
own stand in either one or the other, and not in both.

Against the background of the creative process in general,
Rimbaud's few aphoristic comments about his own work shed
abundant light on the problem of his peculiar contribution to the
poetic enterprise. In the spring of 1871 Rimbaud formulated whatever he was to say on these matters (R, 267-74). The heights of
poetry are described as having been attained at the beginning,
with the Greeks and their vision of the harmonious life, instead of
at the end. "All ancient poetry culminated in Greek poetry, har-

monious Life. From Greece to the Romantic movement—Middle
Ages—there are men of letters, versifiers . . . In Greece, I have
said, verses and lyres, rhythms: Action. After that, music and
rhymes are games, pastimes." Since the beginning, poetry has been
academic and finally moldy. In the end, the Romantics succeed in
arriving at a triumphant failure. They ground their poetry in the
ego of man, thus inculcating the assumption that the purpose is
to enthrone the self. He, Rimbaud, holds that the poet knows
himself in order to make himself a visionary, and that the poet
becomes a visionary by means of a "long, immense and calculated
disordering of *all the senses.*" He thus confronts the unknown,
bringing hitherto unknown forms and "unforms" into play for this
purpose. He takes charge of humanity, even of animals. "Poetry
will no longer accompany action, but *will lead it.*" The Romantics
come close in their emphasis on the responsibility of the soul, but
fall short inasmuch as they attempt to recapture the spirit of the
dead rather than envision the invisible and hear the unheard. And
therefore, Rimbaud concludes, "I am laboring to make myself a
seer."

What is challenging in Rimbaud's wild and shrill remarks
is the proposal that any new poetic insight must run counter to
traditional development and must institute a more original relationship between form and content. Greek poetry gives form to
content as it presents itself in all its vivaciousness to the poetic faculties of man. Subsequent poetry devotes itself increasingly to the
involuted task of singing variations on form itself. It eventually cul-
minates in the hopeless task of trying to resuscitate its own history
rather than turning directly toward content in all its intrinsic newness.

The present task is, according to Rimbaud, to develop a new
style of poetry suitable for moving in upon the content of human
experience: the unknown, the unseen, the unheard. Such content
can arise in the poetic enterprise of formulating experience only
when it is allowed to assume a primacy over form. This reversal of
primacy is to be achieved by a "disordering of all the senses" which
is, be it noted, not at all a function of flippancy, lassitude, and
lethargy, but rather "long, immense and calculated."[39] The overcoming of rules of order is the overcoming of the primacy of form,
a necessary stage in the poetically formulated experience of content.

The theorist might interpose a number of critical questions at this point. First, how can one know what has been postulated as unknown without destroying its character of being unknown? How can one see the invisible, hear the unhearable? Is not any unified and meaningful experience precisely one in which form and order conquer matter and chaos? Is not poetry precisely *the* human enterprise devoted to composition and formation? Second, granting that there might be some interest in exposing oneself to the elements in all their chaos and without any prominent form, would not such exposure be more surely and easily achieved by means of alcohol, drugs, debauchery in general? Is not poetry a rather precarious and contrived, if not self-defeating medium for disordering the senses?

As theorists in the Western tradition we customarily assume that only that can be articulated which has form. We suppose that if anything is initially chaotic, it makes sense only at the moment of its formation. Thus any claim for a primacy of the unformed, unknown, unseen, unheard over the formed, the known the seen, the heard is immediately classified as foolishness (self-contradictory), mysticism (mere privacy), or both—and in any event unsusceptible of being developed in any form, let alone articulated. We see the results today: the primacy of human machination, technology, science. And what is nihilism but the unsupported and unsupporting assertion of form, the articulation of meanings conquering all nature—everything in the path of human "progress" — only to appear senseless, devoid of any integral meaningfulness for man?

The justification for concentrating on form derives, however, from the experience of labor and not at all from the experience of art. In the midst of a labor a man recognizes that his task is to instill order, to form materials. Left unleashed, the propensity to form leads naturally to the present day prevalance of technology: to despair and nihilism. And yet it is precisely in human labor and technology that the unformed is initially confronted: The unformed is the soil out of which human activity grows; it is the soil which supports and nourishes the human enterprise. For the human enterprise is ultimately meaningful, as distinct from articulating meanings, when the human powers of formation are brought to bear upon the materials to be formed in such a way that the whole is preserved. This whole comprises both the mani-

fold of forms *and* the chaos being formed. Human labor and technology do not themselves preserve this whole, since they represent
the formative power only. Here, where the human enterprise leaves
off as a fragment, the poetic enterprise begins: its function is to
preserve the whole in which man confronts content. The poet is
then confronted with form: his job is to re-form this form and
make it true to its content. Since man has of late proven the otherwise uncontested efficacy of form as a principle in itself, the task
of re-forming form to preserve the confrontation with content appears initially negative: it appears to be a matter of contesting particular forms and even the whole principle of form, or at least
loosening up the rigidity associated with the formative powers of
man.

    This brings us to the second critical question. There are,
to be sure, many ways of "disordering the senses," not the least
of which (because most easy) are alcohol, drugs, and general debauchery. No doubt there are useful lessons to be learned from
these ancient and timeless indulgences. But they fail to come to
anything. Alcohol and the like do not lead to a whole in which
form is related to content. They only lead to a glimpse into the
"other half," a glimpse which may in turn occasion an eventual
integration, but may just as easily leave human experience completely bisected and alienated: empty powers of formation (mere
routine), on the one side, powerless confrontation (dissipation),
on the other side. In contrast to these indulgences, poetry remains
committed to form. The poet "is responsible for humanity, even
animals; he has to make his inventions felt, touched, heard," says
Rimbaud (R, 271). The experience of chaos achieved by disordering all the senses is but a part of the project: the whole is accom
plished only in the actual presentation of sensation, of immediate
content. For disordering itself does not allow of a presentation of
sensation: it not only destroys the rutted patterns of merely formal labor but also destroys itself, making one literally insensitive.

    Traditionally, the task of the poet was that of articulating
an experience of formation: displaying, and in this sense "proving,"
the victory of form. This tradition was viable so long as man continued to be sensitive to the recurrent upsurge of content, the encounter with otherness, the confrontation with unform. The poetry
projected by Rimbaud does not deny this tradition its own relevance. In fact, "it will at bottom still be Greek poetry in a way,"

he writes (R, 272). However, the new task of the poet surpasses the old one. It is to articulate a formation while at the same time ensuring the continuance of the experience of unform. For a poem is an order by the very fact that it is *a* poem. The supreme test of Rimbaud's project is to see if a poem can also embody and pre-serve an experience of *disorder*. We turn to one of his, *"Mouve-ment,"* contained in the collection *Les Illuminations* (R, 201-202).[40]

MOUVEMENT

Le mouvement de lacet sur la berge des chutes du
    fleuve,
Le gouffre à l'étambot,
La célérité de la rampe,
L'énorme passade du courant
Mènent par les lumières inouïes
Et la nouveauté chimique
Les voyageurs entourés des trombes du val
Et du strom.

Ce sont les conquérants du monde
Cherchant la fortune chimique personnelle;
Le sport et le confort voyagent avec eux;
Ils emmènent l'éducation
Des races, des classes et des bêtes, sur ce vaisseau
Repos et vertige
A la lumière diluvienne,
Aux terribles soirs d'étude.

Car de la causerie parmi les appareils, le sang, les
    fleurs, le feu, les bijoux,
Des comptes agités à ce bord fuyard,
—On voit, roulant comme une digue au-delà de la
    route hydraulique motrice,
Monstrueux, s'éclairant sans fin,—leur stock d'études;
Eux chassés dans l'extase harmonique,
Et l'héroisme de la découverte.

Aux accidents atmosphériques les plus surprenants,
Un couple de jeunesse s'isole sur l'arche,
—Est-ce ancienne sauvagerie qu'on pardonne?—
Et chante et se poste.

MOVEMENT

The zigzag movement on the banks of the falls in the
     river,
The vortex at the sternpost,
The swiftness of the rail,
The vast passade of the current
Carry through unprecedented lights
And chemical novelty
The voyagers surrounded by waterspouts of the vale
And of the strom.

These are the conquerors of the world
Seeking personal chemical fortune;
Sport and comfort voyage with them;
They carry off the education
Of races, of classes and of animals, on this ship
Repose and dizziness
In diluvain light,
In terrible evenings of study.

For from the talk amidst the machinery, the blood, the
     flowers, the fire, the gems,
From the excited calculations of the fugitive ship,
—One sees, rolling like a dyke beyond the empowered
     hydraulic course,
Monstrous, endlessly iluminating,—their stock of
     studies;
They, driven into harmonic ecstasy,
And the heroism of discovery.

In the most startling of atmospheric accidents,
A youthful couple holds itself aloof on the ark,

—Is it pristine shyness that people pardon?—
And sings and stands guard.

The first dimension of form is provided by the image of the poem taken as a whole. Although more than one reading might well be required in order to extract the picture from the poetic syntax, the forthcoming "story" is simple enough: Voyagers are being conducted on a boat through a valley confronting them with a wide variety of natural vicissitudes. These are no ordinary people but the conquerors of the world, having at their disposal and by virtue of their study, the wisdom of the world. What one sees is not just the tumult of the boat and its environment but also the results of these people's studies. Finally, and in a note of contrast, the poem depicts a lone, youthful couple singing and standing guard.

The image providing the first dimension of the poem is given breadth by the sequence of its presentations. The presentation of an image can be endlessly additive, as images in ordinary, practically oriented discourse necessarily are. We usually stop filling in the details of an image at the moment when some external consideration deems it unpractical to proceed further. The poetic image, on the other hand, has to achieve a unity, and so a termination, by virtue of internal considerations. In Rimbaud's poem the second dimension, the presentation of the image, is provided by the sequence of the stanzas: rather than adding more of the same, each stanza comes at the image from a completely different direction. The first one describes how various kinds of movement are conducting the voyagers through various elements of nature. The second stanza describes not the passage of the ship but the people on the ship. The third stanza unifies the first two. It describes neither the ship nor its cargo of passengers but, having already depicted them, it transcends (negates and yet preserves) these descriptions by reverting to what one sees. It is as though what one sees is not the boat and its passengers, but the stock of studies issuing from these two. It is the meaning of the scene, not just the scene itself. Thus at the end of the third stanza we are diverted from any expectation of further pictorial description. What we then expect is a consideration of the meaning of the whole. This expectation could in turn lead to extrinsic considerations—

say, a theoretical explanation of the meaning of the scene or perhaps a line of connection between the depicted scene and some familiar sentiment. If the expectation were fulfilled, the poetic form of the poem would be destroyed, since the presentation would no longer comprise an intrinsic unity. It is the fourth stanza which masterfully rounds out the articulation, secures the second dimension, and makes the presentation into the poem that it is. This foreshortened stanza calls our attention with utmost clarity to one particular and immediately intelligible part of the scene: a young couple, isolating themselves on what is now called the ark, singing and standing guard. Only one sentiment is expressed about these two—that they are shy in a way wild animals are shy of human beings, and shy in a manner that is long established and presumably justified. But this sentiment is not directly predicated of the couple. We consider it from the standpoint of the narrator asking a question about it: is this the sort of thing which is pardoned? Through this peculiar device the narrator expresses the sentiment and conveys it to the reader; it does not directly belong to the concerns of the young couple, they engage in something else: they sing and stand guard. Thus the stock of studies, rather than issuing in something outside the scene portrayed, in effect, issues in the act of participating in the scene. We are turned back into the formed articulation with breadth and unity: a poem.

The experience of a poem traditionally receives its third dimension from rhythm punctuated by rhyme. This traditional device carries the formative power of the articulation from the semantic level of articulation down to the phonetic, giving the whole a depth it would not otherwise have. The reader is traditionally aided in his passage into a poem by the undulation of matching verses. From the rhyme scheme he receives and retains an abiding foretaste that prefigures the form he subsequently perceives in the image and its semantic wholeness. In France Rimbaud was the first to violate this tradition decisively. We ask why he wrote differently, that is, what it was he accomplished by this act of violence, and all the more because we know that he had complete mastery of the traditional techniques. This poet, hardly more than a boy when he stopped writing, had at the age of fifteen proved he was entirely fluent in the composition of verse, in Latin as well as in French. Unlike many disciples of the free verse he inaugurated, he might just as easily have written in the accepted meter with masculine and feminine rhymes. He was not only in a position to choose; he actually created the alternative. A man only creates and chooses an alternative with some definite effect in view. What was, and what is, this effect?

Rimbaud's free verse undoes what traditional versification would have done. Formative power is not carried from the level of meaning and imagery down to the phonetic level of articulation. The institution of form goes no further in this poem than the division of the sequence of images into semantic units, into verses. Many of Rimbaud's poems, his proses poems in both *Une Saison en enfer* and *Les Illuminations,* do not go this far. In the case of *"Mouvement"* a semblance of rhythm is retained by the versification. The effect of its retention is not to pair off the verses in a phonetic articulation, but to force attention onto the meanings themselves, onto the semantic dimension *in depth.* In *"Mouvement"* each stanza has a meaning (the first is a description of the passage, the second of the passengers, and so on), and each verse constitutes an element in a subset of verses and comprises as well its own manifold of semantic elements. The third dimension, that of depth, is achieved by the deliberately limited form of free verse. An uncompromising force is instituted which focuses our attention onto the detailed content of the articulation.

The poetic character of the poem could easily have been destroyed at the second dimension by a lesser poet's inability to compose a fourth stanza turning our attention back into the situation depicted by the poem. The poem could also have been easily destroyed if Rimbaud had inserted at this third dimension a manifold of familiar and well-adjusted meanings. The poem could thus have been reduced to a clever story or a sentimental reminiscence. As the poem stands, though, attention is called to and fixed upon chaos bounded within form. The three dimensions of form are not only compatible with the chaos of content but they actually gather up the attention necessary to precipitate an experience of the unformed elements.

The eight verses of the first stanza take the form dictated by traditional grammar inasmuch as the first four comprise a compound subject followed by a verb and a complex direct object: the movement, vortex, swiftness, and passade carry the voyagers through lights and novelty. The movement, however, is associated not with the boat, the falls, or the river, but with the banks. The vortex (abyss, whirlpool) is situated, not as an attractive or disruptive force, but as a driving and guiding force at the rudder of the ship. The swiftness is predicated not of the ship or of the water but of the rail on the ship. The current of the water is described not as having direction, no matter how ill-defined, but as being a passade, not as passing on to a goal but as passing back and forth at the same location. These four elements comprise the power conducting the voyagers on their journey.

Each element contains within itself an apparently impossible contradiction. We are not considering traditional images of poetic association which bring out hidden relations: as when, from an easy association like "he moved swiftly on to the next . . . ," we derive poetic phrases like "he moved with swiftness of foot . . . " or "with swiftness of spirit . . . ." The verses in Rimbaud's poem contain elements which work against each other, not insights into elements hitherto unperceived. They do not cancel each other out, as mathematical and logical contradictories do. They contradict each other in the sense that the experience of one (of movement while on board ship, say) is ordinarily opposed to the experience of the other (of the banks in the same situation). That is, for the practical and even the theoretical purposes of any ordinary situation, we take the banks as stationary and the ship as moving; the sternpost as the location of propelled guidance; the rail as one of the few stable and reliable elements of the experience; and the current as having at least some direction. In this stanza our practical and theoretical perceptions are reversed.

Yet if we succeed in letting loose of our preconceptions, we can as a matter of fact experience things in the manner systematically stipulated by these verses. Once we have made ourselves at home on board ship and freed ourselves from the nostalgias and standards of the landsman, the banks *do* move up and down as though forming a lacework. And it is the vortex at the sternpost which does propel the ship. Similarly, whether or not swiftness can be predicated of the rail (or ramp: the confusion of context makes it impossible and irrelevant to determine which) depends upon the position of the observer. Finally, from the standpoint of one looking over the side of the ship, what might be from one point of view a passage of current is from another point of view like a passade. All of these contradictions make sense, then, not because they dissolve themselves into hidden insights, but because we ourselves assume the varying standpoints required to allow the associations to be meaningful. If and when we succeed in doing this, we experience movement and chaos: movement in everything which we ordinarily take to be static, and chaos in our stance.

In whatever way the conflicting meanings of the first four verses are met, it remains to tie them in with the verb "carry." What leads here is movement and chaos itself: not a lighthouse, not human powers of intellection. The voyagers are led through lights, through things illuminated that have never been heard of before, and through a novelty which is "chemical," that is, which has to do with the rearrangement of elements otherwise familiar. Examples of such lights and such novelty are given in the first four verses. The situation there portrayed is reasserted in the last two verses of the stanza: the travelers remain in the midst of the chaos with the water coming at them from all directions and situating them at the center of the "strom" (a Germanic term referring to a flowing stream and recalling, in conjunction with the second verse, the violence of a maelstrom). The travelers are not led beyond this chaos, they are led *into* it.

The eight verses of the second stanza describe in nearly traditional propositional form the human elements on board ship. They are conquerors; they have sport and comfort at their disposal; they embody education; and they work in a specified medium. However, each verse promotes the strangeness of conflicting meanings already experienced in the first stanza. It is contrary to our expectations to have the human elements on board such a ship named conquerors. No indication is given at any moment of the poem that the voyagers have achieved the slightest mastery over the natural elements tossing the ship about. Indeed, the chaotic elements are described as carrying or leading the voyagers, who are themselves overwhelmed rather than victorious. This could be a cases of bad style: the poet telling us something rather than showing it to us. But, the remaining verses reveal a certain consistency of purpose, a reason to their madness.

These so-called conquerors are seeking "personal chemical fortune." Whether or not we can consider them to be truly conquerors depends upon whether we can experience them as fulfilling their search. The "fortune" they seek is not defined directly in the poem. Presumably then its meaning is shown to us rather than told to us. But, as mentioned before, the poem at no point describes the adventurers as coming into possession of anything. Are we as readers then to assume the meaning of the term according to our own whims? If so, we draw upon meanings which lie outside the defining scope of the poem. And since this term describes the purpose of the whole voyage, the appeal to an extrinsic meaning would vitiate the poetic quality of the articulation, the quality of enclosing meanings into an intrinsic whole. In the first instance, we do indeed draw upon the more or less whimsical meanings already familiar to us, but in the crucial case of the term "fortune," as in other cases, the familiar meaning is transformed by the poem as a whole and our first appeal is redirected in its force: we think, for instance, of buried treasure, but we are confronted with chaos. The term "fortune" is of course more directly related to the element of chance, the unforeseen, that which falls into no pre-established pattern. Finding a buried treasure is merely one kind of fortune, a rather whimsical one at that. Thus the voyagers seek fortune—and they have, according to the first stanza, already found it. Given the primordial sense of fortune as that which continuously escapes form, they are still finding it. It cannot be possessed; it can only be confronted. Such is the nature of chaos, and such is what qualifies it as "personal" and "chemical." Only the individual can enact and consummate such an experience and, like the "novelty" of the first stanza, what is thus experienced is a whole manifold of elements rather than merely one element out of tune with the rest. The voyagers do indeed qualify as conquerors, but in a sense running contrary to the traditional one.

What is intimated in the first two verses of the second stanza gathers momentum in the remaining verses. In the midst of this chaos the voyagers are described *not* as frantically attempting to bring the ship under control. Rather, their milieu is one of sport and comfort. They do not have to work to achieve these: they voyage already with them. Then, too, these conquerors are *not* just lounging about: their task is to carry off whatever can be learned about and by various kinds of men at various stations, even about and by sub-human elements. Just what it means, to "carry off education," becomes clear only in the third stanza. Its immediate meaning is described in the three last verses: for the voyagers the task means both repose and dizziness, exposing themselves both to the scouring and cleansing light of day and to the enclosing and obscuring evenings of study. The task itself bears with it the quality of what is encountered: contradiction.

Taken as a whole, the second stanza gives rise to a faint recollection of the biblical myth of the Deluge. This recollection serves to incorporate a familiar meaning into the thrust of the poem. But while the traditional procedure in such cases is to modify the reference in order to enclose it in the experience of the poem, Rimbaud has contradicted the meaning of the myth and so leaves hardly more than an intimation of it enclosed in the poem. Whereas the original myth depicts the salvation of prototypical forms, the obliteration of chaos, and the possibility of a new beginning, here the second stanza bestows primacy upon sporadic movement, focuses attention upon the chaos, and takes as origin and beginning precisely what the Deluge washed away as despicable wastage. The effect of this reversal of familiar meanings is once again to promote the experience and retention of the chaotic elements as chaotic even though bounded within the poem.

The six verses of the third stanza claim that what we actually see in the portrait is a stock of studies. However, these studies are not seen in storage, as the English commercial term "stock" might imply. Rather, the stock of strange studies is seen to be issuing from the talking that belongs right in the thick of the non-related elements: machinery, blood, flowers, fire, and gems— and from the human effort expended to come to terms with these elements—in excited calculations. The education being "carried off" in the second stanza is perceived at the moment of its emergence, issuance, becoming. The "stock of studies" remains linked to, rooted in the chaotic elements and events giving rise to the "education."

The perception of emergence barely captured by the basic structure of the syntax, is secured by the one and only instance of analogy in the poem: the stock issues "rolling like a dyke beyond the empowering hydraulic course." Instead of recalling a comparison with some more familiar mode of emergence, Rimbaud's choice of analogy fixes attention upon the fundamental rule already engendered within the poem. It is not the ship that rolls: the dyke rolls—as indeed it does from the standpoint of the ship. Moreover, the dyke is situated beyond the course of the ship, and although this is reasonable enough, the qualifications laid upon the "course" again exemplify the rule of contradiction. The course of the ship is "hydraulic," recalling the water on which the ship is sailing and also suggesting that the course is not so much the abstract plan of procedure as the surface on which the ship is sailing. It is also "empowering"; that is, the water rather than the wind in the sails provides the driving and sustaining force of movement. This imagery again has some truth to it, but only to the extent that we are driven to acknowledge the primacy of the elements encountered in an enterprise over the theoretical and practical interests giving extrinsic definition to it. And, in the final two verses of the stanza, this is just what the poem drives the voyagers to do; we perceive them being driven into this situation, not undertaking it for their own interests.

The salient character and striking force of the last brief stanza lie in its simplicity. Semantically and syntactically the stanza taken by itself does no violence to our expectations. A young couple, possibly lovers, stand apart at the moment of an atmospheric accident and, keeping careful watch on the situation, respond to the elements with a song. A calm poise is accentuated by the gentle interruption of a comment interjected from the outside. The comment, issuing from an impersonal source and taking the form of a question rather than an assertion, suggests that the stance of the couple is that of "pristine shyness," that is, a long-established habit of withdrawal. The qualification, however, is not asserted by the couple themselves who are, according to the qualification as well as the other verses of the stanza, thoroughly immersed in the situation. The overall effect of the couple's stance is that of repose. The four verses of this concluding stanza then provide the axis allowing the whole poem to present and articulate movement, as the title claims it is doing. For no other axis of movement is given: neither goal nor purpose nor land nor water is perceived as providing the measure necessary to experience movement as movement.

The last reposeful stance anchoring the entire poem is depicted as one directed solely toward the chaotic elements. It is true that the couple are seen as isolating themselves, but there is not the slightest indication that this isolation is the traditional stoical one: they withdraw not from the vicissitudes of the situation but from the others who ordinarily assume some of the burden for dealing with chaotic elements. They withdraw in order to sing and stand guard. A lesser poet at this juncture might have depicted the lovers fondling each other in defiance of their situation. He might also have decribed their enclosed state of consciousness in the midst of the alien elements. Or he might have passed judgment on their relative successes and failures. But in *"Mouvement"* there is no attempt to secure a location where form, finally if only momentarily, prevails. The repose is integral to the encounter with the elements. For to sing is to articulate and celebrate, and to stand guard is to accept the situation as one's own and to focus attention on what arises by chance within it.

The semantic structures of *"Mouvement"* are identical with the normative structures of any human labor. If any instance of human labor is to be meaningful, it must introduce form, not in order to subdue chaos but in order to articulate and celebrate, to accept and observe the situation of chaos.

A short biographical note may help us to understand better the experience of Rimbaud. It is well known that he wrote no more poetry after he was nineteen years of age (R, XXI-XXVIII). He became something of an adventurer, walking north and south through Europe and ending up in Africa, where he engaged in business which took him into exotic territories, some never seen before by a European, others unknown and uncharted. He died at the age of thirty-seven after contracting a tumor in his right knee. Interpreting his life in terms of his poetry, the only viable direction of interpretation, we can surmise that he continued "laboring to make himself a poet." Not that he was preparing himself to write more poetry; only a psychologist would hazard such an inference. But the basic meaning of being a poet does not lie in the ability to produce poems. It lies in articulating and celebrating, accepting and observing. His failure to write poems, in the light of his continued confrontation with chaos according to the self-effacing forms of ordinary labor, is the kind of failure that ennobles because it stems from a profound recognition and thoroughgoing acceptance of the task that lies before one. In Rimbaud's case, chaos was to prevail over and yet to be preserved by form.

notes

The following abbreviations are used:

B.: Charles Baudelaire, *Oeuvres complètes,* Edition de la Pléiade (Paris, 1961); M.: Stéphane Mallarmé, *Oeuvres complètes,* Edition de la Pléiade (Paris, 1961); R.: Arthur Rimbaud, *Oeuvres complètes,* Edition de la Pléiade (Paris, 1963).

All references to these works are cited in the text by abbreviation and page number.

All translations from French and German are ours.

1. Martin Heidegger, *Erläuterungen zu Hölderlins Dichtung* (Frankfurt am Main, 1951), pp. 7-8.
2. G.W.F.Hegel, *Aesthetik,* 2d ed., based on 1842 ed. (Frankfurt am Main, n.d.), 1:22.
3. Ibid.
4. John Dewey, *Art as Experience* (New York, 1958), pp. 5-6.
5. Martin Heidegger, *Holzwege* (Frankfurt am Main, 1957), p. 66.
6. In *Unterwegs zur Sprache* (Pfullingen, 1959), pp. 121-122, Heidegger defines hermeneutic thus: "The expression 'hermeneutical' derives from the Greek word *hermeneuein.* This word is related to the noun *hermeneus,* which can recall the name of the Greek god *Hermes* in a play of thought more committal than scientific rigor. Hermes is the messenger of the gods. The message he brings is that of destiny. So *hermeneuein* is that presentation which makes something manifest insofar as it is

able to hearken to a message. Such a presentation becomes an exposition of what is already said by the poets, those who are themselves already 'the messengers of the gods' according to Plato's dialogue *Ion* (534 e)."

7. Baudelaire (Paris, 1947), p. 119.
8. *Baudelaire, A Collection of Critical Essays,* ed. Henri Peyre (Englewood Cliffs, N.J., 1962), p. 167.
9. Albert Camus, *Discours de Suède* (Paris, 1958), p. 56.
10. Ibid., p. 54.
11. For a discussion of Baudelaire's indebtedness to Poe regarding his theory of the imagination, see *Baudelaire on Poe,* ed. and tr. L. and F. Hyslop (State College, Pa., 1952), pp. 23 ff.
12. Charles Baudelaire, *Correspondance générale* (Paris, 1917), 2:233.
13. Paul Valéry, *Variété V* (Paris, 1945), p. 113.
14. See "Mallarmé's Poetic Transformation" pp. 67 ff.
15. See "Rimbaud's Departure" pp. 91 ff.
16. Translated by Arthur Waley in *170 Chinese Poems* (London, 1926), p. 60.
17. Cf. Immanuel Kant, *Kritik der Urteilskraft* (Hamburg, 1959), §9.
18. Cf. *"Der Ursprung des Kunstwerkes"* in *Holzwege.*
19. Stéphane Mallarmé, *Correspondance 1862-1871* (Paris, 1959), p. 270.
20. Roland Barthes in *Le Degré zéro de l'écriture* (Paris, 1964), pp. 45-46, interprets the trends initiated in contemporary poetry by Mallarmé in the same way: " . . . contemporary poetry has destroyed the relationship of language and it has reduced discourse to stations of words . . . these poetic words exclude men."
21. Mallarmé, *Correspondance,* p. 278.
22. See also Mallarmé, *Oeuvres complètes,* p. 664: "Basically we consider the contemporary epoch as an interregnum for the poet who does not have to get mixed up in it: this epoch is too archaic and too preparatorily turbulent, thus he has nothing else to do but to work mysteriously in view of later or of never and from time to time he should send to the living ones his calling card, in the form of some stanzas or some sonnet, so that they will not lapidate him if they suspect him of knowing that they don't exist."

23. Jean-Pierre Richard, *L'Univers imaginaire de Mallarmé* (Paris, 1961), pp. 231-33, gives a full bibliographical statement about existing works of Hegelian parallels in Mallarmé. He states: "It is certain that between 1866 and 1871 Mallarmé underwent a profound Hegelian crisis, which is visible in the vocabulary of his letters and of *Igitur*."

24. Mallarmé, *Correspondance*, pp. 220-21.

25. Ibid., p. 259.

26. Note also Mallarmé's comments on "authenticating silence" in *Oeuvres complètes* (p. 387). Roland Barthes in *Le Degré zéro de la littérature* says of Mallarmé's language: "the writing of Mallarmé postulates a silence . . ." (p. 67).

27. Henri Mondor, *Propos de Mallarmé sur la Poésie* (Paris, 1946), p. 118.

28. G.W.F. Hegel, *Phänomenologie des Geistes* (Hamburg, 1952), p. 229: "Language and Labor are modes of expression in which the individual no longer keeps within and possesses himself, but allows the Inner to get completely outside himself and gives this over to the Other."

29. Although Wallace Fowlie, *Mallarmé* (Chicago, 1962), p. 223, points out that "the words are absolute in Mallarmé's poetry," he does not mention that poetry issues from the nothingness, the meaninglessness of the world.

30. Roland Barthes, *Critique et vérité* (Paris, 1966), p. 49.

31. J. H. Plumb, ed., *Crisis in the Humanities* (Baltimore, 1964), p. 73.

32. Hegel, *Aesthetik*, p. 22. For a penetrating discussion of the historical shift in the significance of art, see Walter Bröcker, "Hegel's Philosphie der Kunstgeschichte," in his *Auseinandersetzungen mit Hegel* (Frankfurt am Main, 1965).

33. Mallarmé, *Correspondance* (Paris, 1959), p. 137.

34. Jean-Pierre Richard, *Onze Etudes sur la poésie moderne* (Paris, 1964), p. 8.

35. See Nietzsche, *Jenseits von Gut und Böse* (Stuttgart, 1964), §58, and *Zur Genealogie der Moral* (Stuttgart, 1964), Third Essay §18; both have prefaces dating from the late 1880's.

36. Johannes Gottfried von Herder, *Sprachphilosophie* (Hamburg, 1960), p. 24: "Man shows reflection, when the power of his soul acts so freely that within the ocean of perceptions it can distinguish a wave . . . . *This first characteristic of thinking*

was a word of the soul! With it human speech was invented!"
37. Ibid., pp. 35-36: *"For what was this first speech but a collection of elements of poetry? . . . A dictionary of the soul, which is simultaneously a mythology and a marvelous epic of the actions and language of all creatures!"*
38. Igor Stravinsky, *Poétique musicale* (Paris, 1952), pp. 36-37.
39. See "Rimbaud's Departure," pp. 91 ff.
40. *"Mouvement"* because of some descriptive analogies might remind one of Poe's story "The Descent into the Maelstrom." There are, however, important differences between the Rimbaud and Poe pieces. Rimbaud's narrator makes us stand with him in the middle of the maelstrom, at a beginning, moving out into the future. He is opening onto fresh *disclosures* of existence. Poe's old man is released from the whirlpool and relates his past expulsion from the vortex with the wisdom, dread, and reserve of age. He is zeroing in on the *horrors* of existence.

Earlier versions of "Mallarmé and the Experience of Art," "Mallarmé's Poetic Transformation," "Baudelaire and the Experience of Art," and "Baudelaire and the Modern Age" have appeared previously in print: the first in *The Journal of Aesthetics and Art Criticism,* Vol. 30, Spring 1972; the second, under the title "Mallarmé: A New Concept of Poetry" in *The Dalhousie Review,* Vol. 48, Winter 1969; the third, under the title "Baudelaire: An Introduction to Contemporary Art and Aesthetics" in *The Dalhousie Review,* Vol. 52, Spring 1972; the fourth, under the title "Baudelaire: Literary Criticism and the Advent of Technnology" in *Criticism and Culture* (Iowa City, 1972).

selected bibliography

Anderson, John M. *The Realm of Art.* University Park, Pa., 1967.

Barthes, Roland. *Critique et Vérité.* Paris, 1966.

Barthes, Roland. *Le Degré zéro de l'écriture.* Paris, 1964.

Baudelaire, Charles. *Correspondance générale.* Edited by Jacques Crepet. 4 vols. Paris, 1947.

Baudelaire, Charles. *Oeuvres complètes.* Edited by Y.-G. Le Dantec and C. I. Pichois. Paris, 1961.

Blanchot, Maurice. *L'Espace littéraire.* Paris, 1955.

Blanchot, Maurice. *Le Livre à venir.* Paris, 1959.

Bonnefoy, Yves. *Rimbaud par lui-même.* Paris, 1961.

Camus, Albert. *Discours de Suède.* Paris, 1958.

Cohn, R. G. *Towards the Poems of Mallarmé.* Los Angeles, 1965.

Dewey, John. *Art as Experience.* New York, 1958.

Friedrich, Hugo. *Die Struktur der modernen Lyrik, von Baudelaire bis zur Gegenwart.* Reinbek bei Hamburg, 1956.

Fowlie, Wallace. *Mallarmé.* Chicago, 1962.

Heidegger, Martin. *Erläuterungen zu Hölderlins Dichtung.* Frankfurt am Main, 1951.

Heidegger, Martin. *Holzwege.* Frankfurt am Main, 1957.

Heidegger, Martin. *Unterwegs zur Sprache.* Pfullingen, 1959.

Hegel, G.W.F. *Aesthetik.* 2d ed. based on 1842 edition. Frankfurt am Main, n.d.

Hegel, G.W.F. *Phänomenologie des Geistes.* Hamburg, 1952.

Herder, J. G. von. *Sprachphilosophie.* Hamburg, 1960.

Hyslop, L. and F., tr. and ed. *Baudelaire on Poe.* State College, Pa., 1952.

Kant, Immanuel. *Kritik der Urteilskraft.* Hamburg, 1959.

Mallarmé, Stéphane. *Correspondance*. Edited by H. Mondor, J.-P. Richard. 3 vols. Paris, 1959.

Mallarmé, Stéphane. *Oeuvres complètes*. Edited by H. Mondor and G. Jean-Aubry. Paris, 1961.

Maritain, Jacques. *The Situation of Poetry*. New York, 1955.

Mauron, Charles. *Mallarmé par lui-même*. Paris, 1964.

Mondor, Henri. *La vie de Mallarmé*. Paris, 1951.

Mondor, Henri. *Propos sur la poésie*. Paris, 1946.

Nietzsche, Friedrich. *Jenseits von Gut und Böse. Zur Genealogie der Moral*. Stuttgart, 1964.

Peyre, Henri, ed. *Baudelaire, a Collection of Critical Essays*. Englewood Cliffs, N. J., 1962.

Plumb, J. H. *Crisis in the Humanities*. Baltimore, 1964.

Poulet, Georges. *Etudes sur le temps humain*. Paris, 1950.

Poulet, Georges. *La Conscience critique*. Paris, 1971.

Richard, Jean-Pierre. *L'Univers imaginaire de Mallarmé*. Paris, 1961.

Richard, Jean-Pierre. *Poésie et Profondeur*. Paris, 1955.

Richard, Jean-Pierre. *Onze Etudes sur la poésie moderne*. Paris, 1964.

Rimbaud, Arthur. *Oeuvres complètes*. Edited by R. de Renéville and J. Mouquet. Paris, 1963.

Rivière, Jacques. *Rimbaud*. Paris, 1920.

Sartre, Jean-Paul. *Baudelaire*. Paris, 1947.

Scherer, Jacques. *L'Expression littéraire dans l'oeuvre de Mallarmé*. Paris, 1957.

Starobinski, Jean. *La Relation critique*. Paris, 1970.

Staiger, Emil. *Grundbegriffe der Poetik*. Zurich, 1946

Staiger, Emil. *Die Kunst der Interpretation*. Zurich, 1955.

Stravinsky, Igor. *Poétique musicale*. Paris, 1952.

Valéry, Paul. *Variété V*. Paris, 1945.

Waley, Arthur. *170 Chinese Poems*. London, 1962.